ONE IN A SERIES FROM THE PUBLISHERS OF *PRE-K TODAY*

LEARNING THROUGH PLAY

ART

A Practical Guide for Teaching Young Children

Edited by Nancy-Jo Hereford and Jane Schall

Foreword by Bev Bos

Contributing Writers:

Ellen Booth Church

Merle Karnes, Ed.D.

Karen Miller

Kathy Spitzley

Sylvia Tritch

Sandra Waite-Stupiansky, Ph.D.

Illustrated by Nicole Rubel

Early Childhood Division Vice President and Publisher
Helen Benham

Art Director
Sharon Singer

Production Editor
Katie Corcoran

Consultants
Adele Brodkin Ph.D.
Susan Kleinsinger

Copyright © 1991 by Scholastic Inc.

Published by:
Scholastic Inc.
Early Childhood Division
730 Broadway
New York, NY 10003

ISBN # 49115-6
Library of Congress Catalog Number

CONTENTS

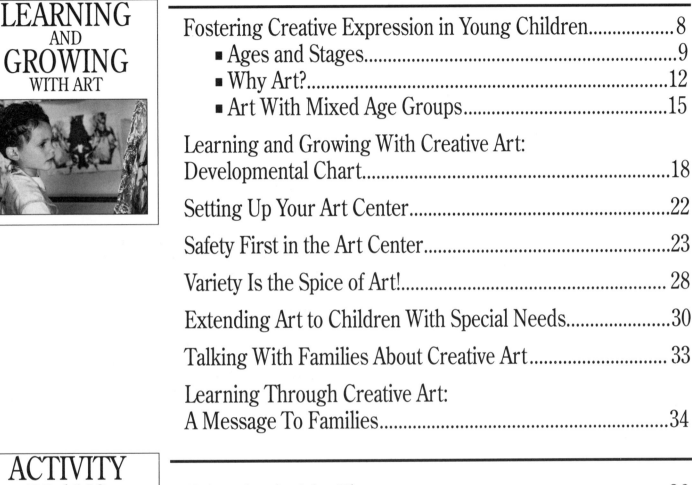

LEARNING
AND
GROWING
WITH ART

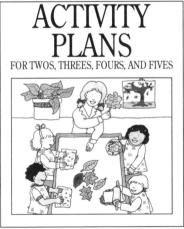

ACTIVITY
PLANS
FOR TWOS, THREES, FOURS, AND FIVES

FOREWORD
A Conversation With Bev Bos:
The Value of Creative Art

Q: What is creative art? And what is its value to children?

A: Creative art is a process. You offer children interesting materials and let them explore. The children at my school, for example, use all kinds of odd items as brushes. When I offer these materials, I have no idea what a child will do with them. I have no product in mind. With a craft project, which is very different from creative art, the teacher has an image of a product the child will create.

I think the greatest value of creative art is its ability to help children become divergent thinkers — to see more than one way to do something, more than one way to solve a problem. Just consider the challenge of a blank sheet of paper. "What am I going to do with this?" the child wonders. "How shall I fill this paper?" Or, "How shall I shape this clay?" "What can I make with these scraps of wood and paper?"

The children who get a solid exposure to creative art will be the problem-solvers of the future — the ones who'll tackle the environment, who'll be the peacemakers. We don't make the connection easily between someone who's very creative and who's also a problem-solver. We think of problem-solvers as logical thinkers, as scientists and mathematicians. There are so many ways to encourage children to think. Creative art is one. And the time to help children develop creative, flexible minds is when they're young!

Q: That's an inspiring reason alone for creative art, but along with helping young children become creative thinkers, in what other ways can they grow through art experiences?

A: They develop physically, of course. All those strokes are early forms of prewriting. Creative art is basic science — colors, shapes, concepts like wet and dry — so they get wonderful exposure to those skills. It also enhances language development.

Q: What about the role of art in enhancing emotional development?

A: Art is a marvelous way for children to express how they feel — be it joy or anger — in constructive ways. When children are creative, you can see feelings coming out. Creative art is also extremely valuable as a means of helping children develop positive self-esteem. You know the number-one condition for self-esteem is uniqueness, but it's not easy for children to feel unique today. Everybody wears the same clothes and enjoys the same toys and activities. Yet with one stroke of crayon on paper, a child can feel special. If children are allowed to express themselves freely, what they create will be different from that of others. They become aware of their own capabilities through the creative process.

Q: We tend to think of art as a solitary activity, but what is its role in encouraging social development?

A: Art can and should be a means of helping children develop socially. As I talk with teachers who attend my workshops, I find one of the most pressing concerns is children's social readiness. We don't live in a casually social world anymore. People don't hang over the back fence exchanging news. Children don't grow up in big families where they have to learn how to negotiate with siblings, how to compromise, and how to make their voices heard. Young children today need every opportunity to develop social skills. I don't mean becoming social butterflies, but being able to interact successfully with others. Research shows that if children don't develop these skills by school age, they have a very tough time.

I've coined a new term — coacting — which I define as a way of interacting with others in a spontaneous way, not necessarily to cooperate to create something together, which we know is tough for young children to do. I look constantly for ways to get children to coact in the art area. We finger-paint side by side on a big table, so hands overlap. I might put up one big sheet of paper where two children can work comfortably, then I let them decide how they'll share that paper. We have a wooden fort outside our school, and small groups of children paint there every day — not as a project, but just enjoying the process of painting, of doing it together. We should never force interaction, but teachers have to think creatively about ways to get children to enjoy art coactively.

Q: What is a teacher's role in helping children benefit from creative art?

A: A teacher first has to understand the value of art and make it available to children every day. In other words, art isn't something you offer on Fridays. To help children get the most from creative art, you have to understand how much better off children are in every way when they have the opportunity to enjoy art on a constant basis.

Teachers also must believe — and communicate to children — that art is something that comes from you, that has meaning for you. It's never judged, it's never graded, and it's never a point of comparison between children or something you make for Valentine's Day. Creative art is one key part of a core of truly child-centered experiences that help to develop young children who are creative thinkers, who are risk-takers, who see boundless possibilities in a blank sheet of paper.

Bev Bos is director of the Roseville Community Preschool in Roseville, California. She is the author of three books: *Don't Move the Muffin Tins*, *Before the Basics*, and *Together We're Better* (all Turn-the-Page Press), and a nationally known advocate for creative art and other developmentally appropriate practices in early childhood programs.

Art is the most intense mode of individualism the world has known.
Oscar Wilde

LEARNING AND GROWING WITH ART

- **FOSTERING CREATIVE EXPRESSION IN YOUNG CHILDREN**

- **LEARNING AND GROWING WITH CREATIVE ART: DEVELOPMENTAL CHART**

- **SETTING UP YOUR ART CENTER**

- **VARIETY IS THE SPICE OF ART! A MATERIALS LIST**

- **EXTENDING ART TO CHILDREN WITH SPECIAL NEEDS**

- **TALKING WITH FAMILIES ABOUT CREATIVE ART**

- **A LETTER TO FAMILIES**

PHOTO: © ERIKA STONE 1991

FOSTERING CREATIVE EXPRESSION
IN YOUNG CHILDREN

Creativity — that flourishing of the imagination — is one of the most important qualities we can help to develop in young children. By providing an atmosphere that nurtures creative thinking and self-expression, you can help children discover the joy of creating and develop a love and respect for the creative spirit within themselves and others.

Art activities are some of the best ways to inspire creativity. They offer children opportunities to explore using stimulating materials, freely express their visions of the world, communicate ideas and feelings for which they may lack the words to explain, and test their power to turn a plain sheet of paper into a creation all their own.

Creative art is also familiar and accessible. You probably have an area of your room already set up with easels, paints, paper, crayons, and other materials children can use to enjoy a range of art activities. Use that foundation and the information, ideas, and suggestions here to help your children's natural creativity flourish!

DEVELOPING THE "WHOLE CHILD" THROUGH CREATIVE ART

As a child's imagination blossoms through art activities, other parts of the child are developing, too. Creative art enhances the whole child — physically, cognitively, socially, and emotionally — in these important ways:

■ *Physically*, children refine control of body movements as they use arm, hand, and finger muscles to create with art materials. Naturally, control varies greatly depending on age and developmental levels. As children grow, their physical development progresses from the head downward and from the shoulders out. Consequently, a two-year-old will not have the same grasp and finger control as a five-year-old. Twos tend toward whole-arm movements, resulting in broad, sweeping strokes when they paint or draw. Through opportunities like those inherent in art, which allow children to experiment with arm, hand, and finger control, most school-aged children acquire the fine-muscle coordination to use conventional writing tools successfully. (For more developmental guidance, see "Ages and Stages," beginning at right.)

■ *Cognitively*, children gain experience with many skills and concepts through creative art. Through experimentation, they learn about line, color, form, shape, and texture. Children also gain understanding of cause and effect as they smear glue on an object and find that it now sticks to other things, or as they mix different paints and get a brand-new color! Children learn about concepts of size — big and little, thick and thin — and also that some activities turn out better when done in a particular sequence. Language skills develop as children describe their artwork orally and in written or dictated stories. Art activities also offer meaningful opportunities to use problem-solving, decision-making, and creative-thinking skills.

■ *Socially*, creative art gives children a setting for learning to cooperate with others. As they share materials or work together on projects, children learn rules for getting along with others. Concepts of "mine" and "yours" become very clear when one child tries to paint on another's paper!

■ *Emotionally*, creative art offers children healthy outlets for strong feelings. They can paint angry pictures or poke and pound clay to work out aggression. Children can work through sadness by drawing a likeness of a family member they miss. And they can experience heightened self-esteem and self-confidence as they proudly complete art projects all by themselves!

For a more detailed review of the most important skills and concepts developed through creative art, turn to the chart, "Learning and Growing With Creative Art," pages 18-21.

EXPLORING BASIC ART PROCESSES

A balanced art program gives children opportunities to engage in each of the processes involved in drawing, painting, printmaking, collage and construction, and modeling. Each of these allows for many variations using different kinds of materials. For example, children might paint with tempera, finger paint, or watercolors on a variety of surfaces. Each type of paint will provide a different kind of experience.

Here is a brief look at each of these basic art processes, focusing on what children are doing and how they develop creatively, as well as physically, emotionally, socially, and cognitively, through each.

■ *Drawing* – From the time children first pick up a crayon, most love to scribble and draw. By giving them the freedom to draw in their own ways and a variety of materials to feed their interests, children's abilities will grow. Often they may start with lines — straight lines, curved lines, fat lines, skinny lines — that go in every direction. Eventually patterns or designs emerge, then shapes connect. By the time children are four or five years old, these shapes may become recognizable objects.

This growing refinement reflects children's developing eye-hand coordination. As they become more adept at making the crayon go where they want it to, children are acquiring fine-motor control.

■ *Painting* – The process of applying streaks of color to a surface is an exciting one for young children. They are discovering that they have the power to change the way something looks! Tempera is the most common paint used in early childhood programs. So that children can discover for themselves how new colors are formed when primary colors mix, start with just the

AGES & STAGES

A child's developmental level will have a major impact on the kinds of behaviors he or she demonstrates in the art area and on the level of sophistication of what she creates. Use these guidelines to help you better understand how your children approach creative art. Remember, of course, that the information is general. Some of your children may demonstrate behaviors more in keeping with younger or older stages.

Two-year-olds

Most twos fall into the random/disordered scribbling stage. It's characterized by these behaviors:
• a lack of motor control and eye-hand coordination
• scribbling for the pure physical sensation of the movement
• lack of direction/purpose for marks
• not mentally connecting own movement to marks on page

Three-year-olds

Many threes fall into the controlled-scribbling stage, characterized by these behaviors:
• improved motor control and eye-hand coordination
• scribbling with control
• involvement in exploring and manipulating materials

- discovery of what can be done with new materials and techniques
- repetition of same actions
- making marks with a purpose and not by chance

Four-year-olds

Many fours fall into the basic-forms stage, demonstrating the following behaviors:

- more developed motor control and eye-hand coordination
- enjoyment of mastery over line
- mastery of basic forms: circle, oval, line, rectangle, and square
- discovery of connection between own movements and marks on page

Five-year-olds

Most fives fall into the pictorial or first-drawings stage, demonstrating these behaviors:

- control over direction and size of line
- advanced motor control and eye-hand coordination
- ability to combine basic forms to create first symbols
- use of art to express personality and relationship to symbols created
- ability to communicate ideas and feelings to others through drawing and other art forms
- ability to name artwork as a form of true communication

primary colors — red, yellow, and blue. Gradually add black, white, and, as your budget allows, special shades and fluorescent paints.

Painting also offers opportunities for older children to develop social skills such as cooperating — by taking turns at the easel and by helping one another with smocks. They also experience heightened self-esteem and self-confidence as they put their own paper on the easel and hang up their finished painting on a drying rack.

■ *Printmaking* – There's a certain "magic" involved for young children in creating prints. When they scratch a design on a soft surface and then make a print of their work, children are often surprised to see the design appear "backward." This element of the unexpected adds intrigue and also builds flexible thinking — a design looks different from different angles! Printing, as a result, becomes an early exercise in seeing something from a different point of view.

Because children generally follow an order of steps to make a print, these activities also help develop sequencing skills. And printing makes it easy for children to indulge in their love of repetition — they can repeat the same design over and over!

■ *Collage (cutting and pasting) and Construction* – Collage and construction are "touching arts" because they require the artist to handle many materials. This emphasis on the tactile is also what attracts children! Building something from household castoffs and making something stick to another surface are fascinating exercises for young children.

An exciting assortment of collage and construction materials offers wonderful avenues for creative expression. There are also opportunities for social growth as children share materials, for physical development as they refine the fine-motor skills involved in cutting with scissors or in manipulating materials, and for emotional well-being as

they announce with pride: "Look what I made!"

■ *Modeling* – Poke, pound, roll! Poke, pound, roll! Modeling with clay, plasticene, or playdough is an active art experience and a sensory one, too. Younger children often play randomly with a material, just enjoying the feel of squeezing it between their fingers or watching it squish when pounded with a fist. Later, as they approach school age, children become interested in making more defined objects. At this stage, avoid any temptation to "assign" a product, such as having everyone make a dish. Instead, offer a variety of materials that encourage children to experiment with interesting effects.

Along with sensory awareness, modeling activities introduce children in a concrete way to "solid geometry" — the concept that shapes can take up space. They also serve an important emotional function, offering children appropriate ways to work through frustration and anger. It's okay to pound and poke at clay. In fact, it's a great release!

OFFERING CHILDREN "OPEN" ART ACTIVITIES

Every art activity should be an opportunity for young children to explore a process, to experiment with materials, to create in their own way by following their own ideas, and to feel successful according to their own measures of success. For this goal to be realized, art activities must be "open" activities.

■ **Open vs. closed** – What makes an activity "open" or "closed"? Open activities are ones with no anticipated results, no right answers against which to judge a child's efforts. Block building, dramatic play, and exploring in the sandbox or at the water table are all open activities that encourage children to draw on their own ideas — to experiment and make endless discoveries.

By contrast, closed activities have an expected result or a right answer.

Asking everyone to make a paper-plate bunny face requires a specific outcome and discourages individual creativity. Another kind of example is a puzzle. There is only one way to arrange the pieces perfectly. There's no room for creativity in putting a puzzle together. But then, enhancing creativity is not the learning goal of a puzzle.

■ **Process vs. product** – In matters of creativity, there is never a right way to make something. When an adult tells a child what to create, he or she communicates that a product is important. At this point there's a risk of failure. In the child's mind, and possibly the adult's, the child's product will either measure up to what the adult expects or it will fall short.

Needless to say, this kind of expectation is very inhibiting to anyone's creativity. When a child draws a turtle, whether at the adult's request or not, and the adult responds with a quizzical "What is it?" or voices concern that the turtle is not green, the child can't help but feel the adult's disappointment, even if the child was pleased with his own rendering. Over time, the child may place less and less trust in his own creative instincts. Art activities become an anxious exercise in trying to measure up, instead of a joyful blooming of creativity and imagination.

But even if the child makes a turtle that the adult oohs and aahs at, overemphasizing product can still be inhibiting. Remember, children's inherent fascination is with the process. The joy of making paper stick together, of splattering wonderfully bright colors of paint on paper, of squishing and squeezing clay is, especially for younger children, the main attraction of art activities. A three-year-old may completely cover a "finished" painting with black paint, just to see the effect. More power to him! The act of sweeping paint across the paper is more exciting than what an adult may see as a "pretty" picture.

When the goal is creativity, total support and encouragement of children's ideas and their execution of those ideas are paramount. Children should feel no risk of failure so that their self-confidence is nurtured along with their imaginations. See the sample introductions that follow for help in gauging your own presentation of art activities to insure that children feel the freedom to create in their own ways.

OPENING THE DOOR TO CREATIVE ART

The language you use can make the difference in whether children feel free to explore an art process or compelled to create a product. Check these sample introductions to art activities to make sure your words communicate that art is an "open," fun exploration for the children in your setting.

■ **Modeling**
Open: "Clay is fun to poke and roll. I wonder what you will do with your clay?" *Closed:* "Can you use your clay to make a cat?"

■ **Painting**
Open: "Here are some bright colors you might like to paint with. Do you think you'd like to use a thick brush or a thin brush?" *Closed:* "Can you paint a nice flower for your mother?"

■ **Collage**
Open: "Let's cut some shapes from this colored paper. I put some paste in this dish. What do you think will happen if you paste the shapes on this black paper?" *Closed:* "Let's use these shapes to make a house. First we can paste a square on the bottom, then a triangle on top for the roof ... then how about a rectangle for the chimney?"

■ **Drawing**
Open: "Here's some drawing paper and crayons. Use as many colors as you like. If you want to describe the colors you use or anything about your drawing, I'll write down what you say or you can write it yourself." *Closed:* "I would like you to color this picture of a girl. Let's give her a red dress, and stay inside the lines."

■ **Construction**

Open: "There are some wonderful materials here — paper towel tubes, little packing pieces, yarn, old buttons, aluminum foil, ... Would you like to use them to make something?" *Closed:* "Remember the story about the Billy Goats Gruff? Well, today we are going to make trolls. Does everybody have a paper towel tube? Let's start by ... "

GATHERING GREAT MATERIALS

As the previous discussion implies, focusing on materials rather than on children's end products is the best way to build excitement and help children to feel comfortable and successful in your art area. Consequently, the choice of materials you offer is critical. If materials are always the same — crayons, playdough, and computer paper — children may feel uninspired. So rather than spending time thinking about interesting projects for children to do, look for interesting materials for them to use. A rich and varied assortment of materials is sure to pique their interest in art.

Also remember the novelty factor. Children are drawn to what is new. Let them experiment with a few new materials to figure out what they are good for and what can be done with them. See "Setting Up Your Art Center," page 22, for basic materials and ideas on more unusual materials to keep art activities new and inviting.

ORGANIZING AND MANAGING ART ACTIVITIES

Art is fun, messy business, especially with young children. The messiness is part of the delight and the source of many important discoveries. While you don't want to limit children in what they can create, it is appropriate to set limits on where they may engage in art activities and on the number of children who can participate at one time.

■ *Set up an art center in your room.* It is critical to provide a specific place where children know they can go to paint, work with clay, do collage, etc. It not only encourages more frequent involvement with art, but lets you plan for the messiness. Choose your oldest table for children to work on, and lay newspaper or oilcloth under easels before children arrive. You can also make a rule that this is the only area where it's okay to sport arms painted up to the elbows! (For more help in arranging or rearranging your art area, turn to "Setting Up Your Art Center," pages 22-27.)

■ *Plan for independence.* Remember, autonomy is an important developmental goal and can be encouraged in many

WHY ART?

As early childhood educators, we know that creative art is an enjoyable activity for most young children. But is it an important one? The late Clare Cherry, author of *Creative Art for the Developing Child* and an educator who firmly believed in the need to nurture the creative core in every child, eloquently answered the question, "Why art?" Her words challenge us to make art the source of wonder, pride, joy, and solace for children that it can and must be.

The art of young children is a celebration of creativity, imagination, and self-expression. Each creation reflects the uniqueness of the child who creates it.

Like a first step taken or a first word spoken, the first marks children put on paper with crayons or paint are made with uninhibited and luxurious abandon. Seeing those marks, the child experiences the profound realization that he or she has the power to change the way his environment looks and that such change can be created on his own terms. This leads to an important understanding — that the child is in control of his own actions.

Art has many benefits for children. Art experiences not only build self-esteem and self-confidence, but the actual physical process is a key component in the development of perceptual and motor skills and of eye-hand coordination. As children experience the use of various materials, cognitive skills are developed. They learn to

ways. Hang smocks on low peg hooks in the art area and, except for the very youngest, teach children to put on their own smocks or to ask a peer for assistance. (Old shirts make fine cover-ups. If your budget allows, commercially available waterproof smocks are great for both painting and water play.) Store materials on low open shelves so children have easy access. (Observing in the art area will help you monitor and avoid potential waste of materials.) Help children learn to get in the habit of putting their own paper on the easel and of taking the finished painting to the drying rack.

■ *Work with small groups.* Rather than initiate an art project for the whole group (which assumes that every child is doing the same project, with the same materials, at the same time), capture children at their creative best. This means offering them time and encouragement to come to the art area on their own, motivated by their own interests. Never force a child to participate in art activities.

■ *Present creative art as an activity choice during free-play periods.* Depending on the size of your art area and on the age of your children, let from two to four children at a time choose art as a play activity. There are several advantages to this system.

Children can work at their own pace, and the atmosphere is more relaxed. They can talk to you and to each other about what they are doing, and you can observe each child more easily. And cleanup with four is a lot less involved!

■ *Use free-play periods to introduce special art materials to a few interested children at a time.* There may be particular techniques you would like to offer children that require more help from you, such as introducing batik. (See "Crayon-and-Paper Batik" Activity Plan, page 63, as well as other ideas for special projects in the Activity Plans section.) Offer each as an alternative activity in the art area, letting children choose to try it if and when they're ready. Working with a few children at a time makes it easier to individualize the project, so that each child does as much as he can.

■ *Plan for "crowd control."* What do you do when your batik process draws a small crowd of children who all want to do the activity at the same time? (Remember the novelty factor!) Start a waiting list, trying roughly to position the names in the order that children asked to do the project. Show each child his name and assure him that this list guarantees a turn. Then, repeat the project the next day and the next as needed

classify, organize, and categorize; they practice solving problems and learn the excitement of experimentation. As they work in the company of other children, they expand their social skills. And as they see the results of their work and that of others, their capacity for aesthetic appreciation grows.

Along with this growth, children gradually become aware of the great opportunities for emotional release and satisfaction that accompany the creative act. They may not understand why, but they become aware that doing art is very satisfying and that it makes them feel good inside.

All of these aspects of creative art have important implications for children growing up today. There are so many uncertainties, so much stress and anxiety, and so much confusion and ugliness. Children need help in

coping with feelings brought about by life experiences they cannot understand or control. Expressing themselves through art and enjoying the sensation of creating can be a powerful means of coping.

Children also need opportunities to know that not everything in life comes predesigned in a box. They need exciting media to touch, to hold, to shape. They need to know that they can be the designers — that they can create line and form where none were before. They need to feel the first stirrings of that innate force that prompts humans to bring beauty into unbeautiful places.

These are critical needs. And they can be met through individualized and developmentally appropriate art programs. Art is not a bonus for young children — it is a necessity.

to accommodate everyone on the list. As long as you follow through, children will relax, knowing that they'll get a turn each time.

■ *Allow for repetition.* You know that young children love to repeat the activities they enjoy. This holds true with art as well. As you organize, plan for repetition. Make sure you have plenty of supplies so that children know they can make another picture, print, or collage if they want. If you have introduced a special process, repeat it at least three times in a week, so that children can try it when they are ready and as often as they want. If it's popular, reintroduce the activity in a few weeks. When you allow children to repeat art activities, whether the chance to paint at the easel or to try something more unusual, you give them time to explore materials in depth and master techniques to their satisfaction.

them see paper, crayons, and paints as "tools" for enhancing other kinds of creative play. For example, a small dramatic-play group might like to make tickets for the "bus to Boston." Children can make signs for block buildings or a hat for a puppet. Organizing your art setup so children feel free to use materials on their own makes it easier for them to use art to expand or respond to other activities.

RESPONDING TO CHILDREN'S ARTWORK

A child brings you a picture he has just created. His face beams with pride. He feels accomplished and wants to share his success with you. How should you respond?

■ *Make an interested and enthusiastic comment about the process or about how the child feels about the project.*

■ *Integrate art into other parts of your program.* Naturally, you want children to see art not as an isolated activity, but as something connected to other activities or events. To help encourage this integrated view, you might ask children if they'd like to paint the colors they remember from a science walk outside or help make a thank-you picture to send to the fire station you visited. Help

In other words, resist giving blanket praise. Comments such as, "That's great!" can become meaningless. A specific yet nonjudgmental comment tells the child that you are really looking at what he has created, and that you care most about how he created it and how the he himself feels about the work. For example:

"I see lots of round shapes over here.

They go from small to big."

"It looks like you had fun with yellow today!"

"I can tell by looking at this picture that you love to paint!"

"It's fun to see how you put these shapes together. I like your ideas!"

What's most important? Accept whatever the child produces. Commenting does not mean you have to evaluate. Most of all, remember: Rather than ask, "What is it?" invite the child to tell you about his work.

■ **Display children's artwork with respect.** When you take the time to attractively display children's work, it communicates to them and to their families that you value their creative efforts. Colorful artwork displayed around your setting adds beauty to your environment as it boosts young artists' self-esteem.

As part of a display, you might include a description of the process, the materials used, and the benefits for children. Ask children if they want their name on their work and where. A child may prefer his name on an index card attached to or tacked near the artwork.

What if a child would rather take a project home than display it? Naturally, never force the child. One strategy is to allow children to repeat an art activity so that each has something to take home and something to display.

Here are ideas for different ways to display children's artwork:

Frame it with special materials. Mat children's art with colored construction paper or with brightly colored burlap, calico, or other fabrics. Buy several inexpensive colorful frames and showcase different children's work every few days. Place matted or framed pictures in the hallways or the lobby of your school or center to add color and interest to communal areas and to provide visitors with information on the creative aspects of your program.

Focus on different processes. As you introduce children to different art processes, save at least one example of each — construction, collage, printmaking, drawing, painting, modeling, etc. Display this collection on a bulletin board or table, along with a description of each process. This is a great way to remind children of all the different kinds of art they've experienced, as well as a way to give families an overview of your program.

Give each child a personal display. If space allows, designate a separate display area for each child. Let each choose one color of paper as the display background, and staple the paper to a wall. Print the child's name on a large card, or let him design his own nameplate, and attach it to the paper. Now let him decide what he wants to show off there. You might expand the display to include his dictated stories and writing.

Put the children in charge. Designate a bulletin board or wall space at children's height as the "group art gallery." Set out masking tape (or thumbtacks for fours and older) and let the children decide what they want to display. This kind of decision-making gives children a feeling of ownership of their room.

■ **Keep examples of children's artwork on file.** Include dated samples of each child's creative work in a personal folder. Over time, this artwork offers one more means of looking at a child's growth. Notice how the child experiments with color and materials. Look for increased control over the direction of lines and the combination of shapes, and for signs that he is starting to represent objects in drawings or paintings. If possible, record his comments about each product or process and your own observations of the child at work. All this information gives you and the family a more detailed picture of his development through art.

OBSERVING IN THE ART AREA

As with every other activity in which children engage, observing budding artists at work is critical. Through obser-

ART WITH MIXED AGE GROUPS

As a family child-care provider, you want your children to be able to engage in art activities. But you have three special challenges:
• accommodating children who represent a range of ages
• providing an interesting assortment of materials without breaking your budget
• protecting your furnishings from messy art activities

With planning, you can meet these challenges and make creative art a much-enjoyed part of children's days with you. Here's how.

ACCOMMODATING DIFFERENT AGES

▼*Keep art projects open-ended.* Don't suggest a product for everyone to make. Instead, provide materials and let children explore and create in their own ways.

▼*Let each child enjoy the same basic activity, but always at his or her own level.* Let's say you've put out a variety of old magazines, paper, glue, and markers for children to use in making collages. Now you can observe how each child responds to the materials, assisting as needed.

The baby sitting on your lap or in an infant seat simply may enjoy being a part of the action. The toddler may just want to turn the magazine pages or, if you have cut out some pictures ahead of time, might paste a few on paper. The preschooler cuts and pastes pictures on her own in random fashion. By contrast, the school-aged child is probably very particular about what she cuts out and where it's placed on the paper. She may use markers to outline the pictures and give her finished collage a title.

▼ *Plan for the occasional cooperative project.* Everyone can work on a birthday banner or tape drawings and objects to a common mural. They can tape and glue boxes and junk materials together, then paint their sculpture. Observe, and then help each child find a role in the group endeavor.

▼ *Establish a daily routine that includes time for art.* It meets a younger child's need for repetition and an older child's need to plan. For all ages, the chance to do art projects every day means that if they don't feel like creating today, they know they can always create tomorrow!

SAVING MONEY ON MATERIALS

Your home environment is rich in materials for creative expression. See "Setting Up Your Art Center," pages 22-27, for ideas on castoffs to collect for art activities. You might also join forces with other family child-care providers in your area to order supplies in bulk at a discount.

ORGANIZING FOR SUCCESS

As a rule, art activities are messy. These organizing tips will help protect your furniture and floors without inhibiting children's creative expression.

▼ *Designate one place in your home for art activities.*

vation, you learn who frequents the art area and who is almost never found there, how individual children are benefitting from art activities, and when the art center is getting "old" and needs an infusion of new materials. There's no substitution for your own eyes and ears in acquiring this kind of important information.

But when you observe, questions or concerns may surface. This section offers guidance in dealing with issues that may arise from your observations.

■ ***Should you interfere when you observe a child doing the same kinds of activities all the time?*** You know repetition is important and appealing to young children. If they like an activity, they can do it over and over with continued enjoyment. Keep in mind that doing one activity well and relishing in it provides some children with the psychological reserves to tackle activities that are tougher for them. Painting a wonderful picture of trees every day may be what one child needs to feel good about himself. Pushing the child to try something new may diminish those reserves of confidence.

However, there are children who get stuck in a rut and may benefit from carefully offered suggestions. The key is to not force the child. Offer ideas in a way that the child can accept or refuse your suggestions. You might say, "What if you added a flower growing near those trees?" or "Would you like to add red to your picture? How do you think it would look with the blue you like?" Or, you might offer to paint a picture with a child who never paints. By gently expanding the child's artistic repertoire, you stimulate ideas without making the child anxious.

■ ***How can you recognize the range of talent among children and still help each to feel good about his own work?*** There is a broad range of artistic talent as well as vast developmental variation in young children. Some will demonstrate amazing creativity while others will lag far behind in fine-muscle con-

trol. Your behavior and reactions act as a model for children's own behavior.

First, be respectful of each child's abilities. Never show a child how to draw something in a more realistic way or how to position materials on a paper. Never finish a project for a child or tell him to stop because you think the project looks "right."

Don't compare children's art with that of others. Instead, help children to measure their work against what pleases them and see ways in which they are improving in skill compared with earlier examples.

Don't be afraid to praise children, stressing, for all children, the things they are good at. Help your group see that everyone excels in something. For some it may be block building, while for others, it's art.

■ ***How can you help children avoid conflicts in the art area?*** As with any other area of the room, there is potential for conflicts here as well. Children may fight over materials. Angry words may erupt when one child accidentally or deliberately destroys another's work. Plan ahead by providing an adequate supply of materials. Limit the number of children who may work in the area at one time, and enforce that limit. Also, involve children in setting a few well-chosen rules for behavior in the art area.

When problems do arise, involve children in arriving at reasonable solutions. For example, two children might decide to work together on a project if there are not enough materials for each to work alone. And occasionally, as in the case of a child who deliberately destroys another's work, you may need to step in and remove the child from the art area. Talk about how engaging in art activities is a privilege and that the privilege will be restored when the child agrees to follow the rules.

■ ***How do you interpret what you see in children's art?*** While it's true that children often use art as a way to express their emotions, be cautious if you attempt to interpret children's artwork. A child who uses lots of black paint is not necessarily depressed or anxious. It may be that black paint has not been available for a while, or the attraction may be the sharp contrast of inky black on white paper. Ask the child to tell you about the picture. His own description will often reassure you that the form or colors used were just interesting to the child, not a sign of problems.

It's also important to always view a child's artwork in a broad context. If a child paints one depressing or disturbing picture, he may just be having a bad day. If everything else about the child seems on track, yet he paints a violent picture, he may simply be responding to an overly graphic television program or movie and trying to work through his confusion. If you know a child has experienced a trauma at home — such as a death or parents separating — he may use art to work out feelings of sadness or anger. Try to look for the obvious and normal reasons why artwork may appear disturbing or depressing before you look for any deep dark reasons that may signal a dysfunctional child or home.

However, don't ignore cumulative signs of trouble. For example, if a child draws disturbing pictures over a period of weeks, describes violent scenes when asked to tell about the pictures, and engages in other kinds of play that seem abnormal for that child, it's time to find out if something is wrong. A talk with family members is the most appropriate action. If you have a counselor or pediatrician affiliated with your school or center, consult this professional for advice. Work through the family in seeking help for the child.

EVALUATING YOUR ART CENTER: IS IT A PLACE FOR EVERYONE?

Is your art area appealing to action-oriented children? Can children find colors of paint to complement the skin types of everyone in your room? Though art should always be a free-choice option, you want all of the children in your room to feel welcome in the center. Subtle messages make a difference. These reminders can help you ensure that your art center is a comfortable, exciting place for every child.

■ Display pictures in the art area of men and women representing a variety of racial and ethnic groups, as well as some with disabilities, involved in creative activities such as art, architecture, and house painting.

■ Use art activities to enhance dramatic play or block building. Painting large boxes and making signs are especially appealing to more action-oriented children.

■ Provide intriguing materials, such as aluminum foil or glow-in-the-dark paints, for children to use.

■ Specifically "invite" a child who rarely visits the art area to try an activity. "Mark, would you like to do an easel painting?"

■ Occasionally move the easels and other art materials outdoors, where children can be loud and expansive.

■ Have a variety of skin shades for children to choose from when they paint or draw people, such as tan and other brown hues as well as lighter skin colors. You can premix shades or show children how to mix colors.

■ Place an unbreakable mirror in the art area, and encourage children to focus on their own skin, eye, and hair colors, as well as those of peers.

■ Some children may put value judgments on colors, stating, "Yuck, black is ugly," or, "I hate brown." There are times when this is an indication of individual preference. However, sometimes it may reflect a child's attitude about skin colors. Help children to see the beauty in all colors.

Karen Miller, special projects editor for *Pre-K Today*, is the author of a number of books for early childhood professionals, co-author of Scholastic's *Learning Through Play: Blocks*, and a contributor to *Learning Through Play: Dramatic Play*.

Children will learn to keep crayons, paste, and playdough on the kitchen table and paint at the easel if these are the only places where art materials are offered and allowed.

Set up your art worktable over hard flooring. Organize supplies on a low shelf near the table. Collage materials can go in a cardboard box or rinsed ice cream bucket. Keep crayons in a basket. Cut holes in the plastic lid of a coffee can for storing blunt scissors.

▼ *Protect your floors.* Place an old vinyl tablecloth or shower curtain under the art worktable and the easel. Have a large sponge ready to wipe paint from the soles of shoes before children track it through the house. Make it a rule that children must wash their hands before leaving your art area.

▼ *Encourage independence.* Having a special container for each item makes it easier for children to find items and help with cleanup. Storing materials on a low shelf makes it possible for children to reach them without having to ask you every time. Put a non-slip stepstool at the sink so they can wash their hands after they finish a project.

▼ *Offer art outdoors.* On a warm day, painting outside and looking for materials to create a nature collage are delightful experiences for children of all ages. And enjoying art outside largely eliminates concerns about the mess!

Kathie Spitzley has been a family day-care provider in Holland, Michigan, for 10 years and is accredited by the National Association of Family Day Care.

LEARNING AND GROWING

Watch a child freely engaged in exploring with stimulating art materials and it's clear that art experiences enhance all areas of development — creative, social, emotional, physical, and cognitive. And the benefits grow as children enjoy a variety of open-ended activities over time, integrated into a well-rounded curriculum.

The skills and concepts identified in this four-page chart are key ones. Each entry begins with a description of how a skill or concept is developed through art experiences. "Ways to Assist" includes ideas on how you can promote further development. "Developmental Considerations" will help you know what to expect from younger (ages 2-3) and older (ages 4-5) children; behaviors vary at all ages, so view these as guidelines only.

Make the most of art by offering opportunities and experiences in a relaxed and encouraging manner, showing children that you also value art for the pure pleasure and satisfaction it brings.

SOCIAL & EMOTIONAL

INTERACTION SKILLS

In a relaxed atmosphere where children feel free to create, social-interaction skills grow. Children naturally exchange ideas, talk about their creations, ask questions, and try out others' use of materials. Observing these exchanges can help you learn much about each child's social development.

Ways to Assist
- Set up your area so that small groups of children can work comfortably together.
- Provide plenty of basic materials so children can work on the same activity without arguing over specific objects.
- Plan for special projects where children can work with each other cooperatively.
- Help children notice others' creations by showing interest yourself, but never compare one child's artwork with that of another.
- Step back and let children test their negotiating skills as they try settling conflicts.

Developmental Considerations
- Twos and young threes are not ready for much interaction. They tend toward parallel play with others, doing the same type of activity in close proximity, but without truly interacting.
- Older threes, fours, and fives are becoming more social. They converse as they work, share ideas, incorporate suggestions from others, and eventually engage in projects cooperatively.

WITH CREATIVE ART

DEVELOPING AUTONOMY

Autonomy is an important developmental milestone. Feeling a mastery of a medium contributes to a growing sense of self and independence. Set up your art center so children can help themselves to materials and clean up on their own to add to this sense of autonomy.

Ways to Assist
■ Furnish art materials that are developmentally appropriate and allow for mastery and challenge — limited choices for younger children and a wider choice for older ones.
■ Place materials on low, open shelves. Use picture labels for each material.
■ Provide child-sized cleanup materials, low sinks, etc., to encourage independence.
■ Don't do for children what they can do for themselves. Let them discover what they can master on their own.

Developmental Considerations
■ Twos and threes will feel more capable when they work with a few materials they can use successfully with minimal help, such as paper, easel paints, and playdough.
■ Older children need materials that afford numerous choices and self-directed projects. Fours are learning to choose materials and return them. Most fives will be almost totally independent in using materials and cleaning up.

POSITIVE SELF-ESTEEM

As children experience the joy and pride of creating artwork that they and others value, they feel good about themselves, their efforts, and their abilities. As they experience success, children are motivated to new and even tougher challenges.

Ways to Assist
■ Offer open-ended activities that let children use their own ideas and feel successful. Trying to conform to an adult model has the opposite effect.
■ Help children realize that they are creating for personal satisfaction, not to please others. When a child asks if you like a creation, you might say, "Do you like it? That's what's really important."
■ Coach family members to respond to children's art in positive, esteem-boosting ways.

Developmental Considerations
■ Twos and threes derive great pleasure from discovering that they can make a mark and change the way something looks! This makes them feel powerful — an important element in developing healthy self-esteem. Carefully redirect children who are working in an inappropriate place, such as scribbling on a wall, so they don't associate guilt with their attempts at creativity.
■ Fours and fives feel pride when they create something that receives positive attention from adults. You need to give this positive feedback without judgment or comparison.

EXPRESSING EMOTIONS

Art is a wonderful outlet for children's emotions. They can express joy and happiness or work through feelings of sadness, fear, or confusion. They can draw a picture of a family member they miss or recall the colors of an exciting autumn walk. For children who are tense, art can offer an appropriate and much-needed release!

Ways to Assist
■ Let children use materials in their own ways. Accept their ideas and what they say about their work.
■ Display children's work with respect to show it's valued.
■ Avoid reading too much into children's artwork. If a child is feeling low one day, he or she may paint a sad picture. Only if the child persists in creating art that seems abnormal for that child should you consider the possibility of a major problem.

Developmental Considerations
■ Younger children have difficulties sorting through the strong emotions they feel, so art can be a good release. The fewer restrictions placed on their artistic attempts, the more satisfaction they'll feel.
■ Fours and fives use color and form to express their emotions, but they're still highly experimental. They may use black because of its power and opaqueness, not necessarily because they're depressed.

LEARNING AND GROWING

PHYSICAL DEVELOPMENT

FINE-MOTOR SKILLS

Art activities offer children meaningful tasks for practicing motor skills. A young child starts with control of only large arm muscles, but in time masters small muscles in wrists, hands, and fingers. The appeal of art translates into many opportunities to refine muscle movements and an incentive to work toward greater control.

Ways to Assist

■ Encourage children to move from larger to smaller spaces as they gain control. For example, suggest painting with water on sidewalks before using easels.
■ Offer materials that are appropriate to children's levels of development. Accommodate the range by providing tools in varying sizes.
■ Don't push children into using materials that require more fine-motor control than they have. Frustration will be high and self-confidence will be lowered.

Developmental Considerations

■ Twos need simple, durable materials and lots of room for whole-arm movements. Be prepared for spills and accidents as a result of undeveloped finger control.
■ Threes begin to control tools with rotations of the wrist instead of the whole arm.
■ Fours and fives show greater finger and wrist control. Practice with fine-point tools and smaller paper will increase dexterity, but most aren't ready to execute well-formed letters or numerals.

COGNITIVE DEVELOPMENT

USING SYMBOLS

As you know, art offers children ways to express their ideas and feelings. In the process, they make connections between what they create and what the shapes or figures signify. This is the beginning of understanding symbols — that one thing can represent another — enabling children to grasp in time that letters and numerals stand for something, too.

Ways to Assist

■ Offer only open-ended art activities so children are truly free to express their own ideas and emotions and take risks.
■ Encourage children to articulate the ideas or emotions they symbolize by asking, "Would you like to tell me about your creation?" Respect a child's right to not discuss the work.
■ Record children's descriptions so they see written symbols for the ideas they express.

Developmental Considerations

■ Twos are discovering that pictures represent real objects. But rather than drawing pictures, they're more interested in exploring with materials. They are not yet ready to follow a plan and are often influenced by others' interpretations of their art.
■ Fours and fives plan their creations, using colors more realistically and beginning to label artwork with their names — acts that let them represent themselves as creators.

LOGIC AND REASONING SKILLS

As art enhances creativity, it also offers opportunities to develop logic and reason. As children decide which colors to mix, how to create a sturdy construction, and how to mold clay, they are reasoning. Through trial and error, they discover properties of materials and physical laws which influence creative decisions and increase their overall understanding of their world.

Ways to Assist

■ At nonintrusive moments, ask a child engaged in a project to talk about what he is doing. This will help you understand his reasoning skills.
■ Encourage children to predict results: "What will happen if you mix these two colors of paint together?"
■ Don't discourage children from following through on a plan that uses faulty reasoning, such as providing an unstable base for a construction. Let the child make discoveries on his own.

Developmental Considerations

■ As twos and threes naturally explore materials, such as dipping the wooden end of the brush into paint, to see how things work, they develop notions of cause and effect which lead to the use of logic and reasoning.
■ As fours and fives begin to form ideas about how the world works, they discover patterns which, with repeated exploration and cognitive maturity, are applied to other situations.

WITH CREATIVE ART

VISUAL/SPATIAL SKILLS

Art is a natural way for children to discover how shapes differ, fit together, and combine. As children begin to discriminate between shapes, they also become more aware of those shapes in their environment. These discrimination skills also prepare children for distinguishing letters when learning to read.

Ways to Assist
- Point out shapes in children's artwork: "I think I see circles in your drawing. Am I right?"
- Discuss shapes in your environment: "Let's find all the circles in our room."

Developmental Considerations
- Twos and threes may incorporate circular scribbles, lines, and dots into their drawings spontaneously. But remember not to ask younger children to deliberately create specific shapes — it is beyond their understanding and ability.
- Fours and fives may use common shapes, like circles and lines, to make people. Once they discover how to make a new shape, they may make it repeatedly, marveling at their mastery. Older children also begin to incorporate notions of size into their figures — Daddy is bigger than baby — though they're still far from using a realistic scale.

USING LANGUAGE

Art activities are wonderful opportunities to enhance language skills. Children who have been allowed to create freely are often excited about what they've made and want to tell you about it. Some will verbalize as they work. Others will wait until their creation is completed. In either case, art is still a spark for encouraging expressive and receptive language.

Ways to Assist
- Be a model by describing the colors and shapes you see in a child's work: "I see red drops on your painting. Would you tell me about them?" Your questions can help prompt the child to express his ideas.
- Display art at children's eye level to encourage them to talk about the work they see.
- Expose children to written language by inviting them to dictate or write stories about their artwork.

Developmental Considerations
- Twos and threes learn words and language rules by modeling others and by having meaningful opportunities, like art activities, to use language. You can provide the words to describe activities: "I see Olivia is painting. She has blue paint and a big brush."
- Fours and fives will verbalize what they plan to make and enjoy telling elaborate stories about their creations.

AESTHETIC APPRECIATION AND CREATIVE EXPRESSION

When children are allowed to create in their own ways, art offers rich opportunities for unleashing imaginations. Children take risks with colors and materials and test ideas that lead to exciting discoveries. They also begin to appreciate the power of creating something to make their physical space more pleasing.

Ways to Assist
- Give children developmentally appropriate, stimulating materials and total creative freedom. A model made by an adult, even if it's just for "ideas," tells them that you have a product in mind.
- Comment on colors, patterns, and use of space in children's art, but don't judge. Asking "How do *you* like what you made?" encourages creating for self-satisfaction.
- Enhance children's awareness of art. Draw their attention to the pictures in books. Display prints by artists that appeal to children.

Developmental Considerations
- Twos and threes care about process, not product. They need simple materials to work with, limited choices, and lots of time to explore materials and techniques and repeat activities they enjoy.
- Fours and fives still gain pleasure from the process, but they begin to show interest in products and may want to start over when they don't like what they make. They begin to see patterns and details in artwork.

Sandra Waite-Stupiansky, Ph.D., is assistant professor at the Center for Teacher Education, the State University of New York at Plattsburgh.

SETTING UP YOUR ART CENTER

Some activities, like dramatic play, find a home in many nooks and crannies in your setting. Others need a well-defined space. Art is one of them. It's messy, yet it's most appealing to children when there's an organized assortment of materials to work with; and it demands "creating room." These are elements that can't be provided for by chance. An area designed for art offers a unique and necessary environment to enhance creative expression.

But, as you know, there's more to setting up an art area than putting up the easels. The decisions you make about where to locate the area, what materials to stock it with, and how to organize those materials greatly influences the quality and frequency of children's par-

ticipation. This section is designed to help you arrange your own art center — or rearrange your existing space — to encourage creativity, independence, and a satisfying semblance of order for everyone!

CHOOSING YOUR LOCATION

Use these considerations as you select a location. They'll help you narrow down your possibilities to one that's closest to accommodating all three.

■ **Traffic flow** – Look around your room during a typical free-play period. Identify the areas of heavy traffic flow. Then try to locate the art space away from these areas. Remember, art by itself tends to be a quieter activity, less compatible with high-energy block building or indoor riding toys. Keeping art out of harm's way also minimizes the chance of accidents and destroyed artwork.

- **Flooring** – An area with vinyl flooring is your best choice. But since traffic flow may be the more important concern, you can use plastic tarps (even old shower curtains) to protect carpeting or other hard-to-clean surfaces.

- **Cleanup** – The closer the art center is to your water source, the easier cleanup will be. But if your art area has to be placed so the sink is across the room, keep a bucket or pan of soapy water and paper towels nearby.

DESIGNING YOUR DREAM CENTER

Dream a little. What would your ideal art area look like? Design it for yourself, then assess reality and cut back as needed. You'll probably want to provide materials, storage, and "creating" space for the basic processes — drawing, painting, printmaking, collage and construction, and modeling. (If you offer woodworking, you might set it up nearby.)

As you envision your setup, you may picture children free to engage in their choice of processes. However, as reality dictates, you may not have the space to allow for this kind of choice. Test different processes to see which are most interesting to the greatest number of children. For example, you may always want the easels up for painting, paper and crayons out for drawing, and playdough available for modeling. Perhaps supplies for making prints or collage and construction materials can be brought out from your storage cupboards a couple of times a week.

As you arrange tables, shelves, and other furniture, evaluate the traffic flow within the art area for potential problems. Place the easels in a corner or mount them on a wall so children and adults won't trip over them. Set up a place close by for paintings to dry, so children don't have to cross the room with wet creations. Designate safe places for other products to dry or to be displayed.

Remember, too, that projects such as group paintings, murals, and box constructions may best be done on the floor. As you arrange furniture and equipment, keep a section open for such activities. As needed, use a plastic tarp, old shower curtain, or vinyl tablecloth to protect flooring.

As you plan, consider how many children will be able to work comfortably in the area at one time. Because children need space to stretch out when they draw, model, build, etc., be conservative in your estimate. Consider how you'll accommodate special art projects, such as those featured in the Activity Plans section of this book, along with the basic processes. You may want to designate a "special projects" table and special shelf space for storing necessary materials. Over a few weeks' time, this table might sport a weaving minicenter, stitchery supplies, and even puppet-making materials, all adding more interest and novelty to the area.

For additional help in setting up your art area, see the illustrated description on pages 26-27.

SELECTING EQUIPMENT AND FURNITURE

- **Tables** – Small circular tables with smooth laminated tops are good choices for art. They fit into small spaces and accommodate the small groups of children who'll be working at one time. If you must use long tables, divide them into separate work spaces using brightly colored fabric tape. For example, one end of a long table might be a modeling work space for two children, while the other end might be a place for drawing.

- **Easels** – One or two freestanding or wall-mounted easels are a must. Cover them with self-stick paper so they'll wipe clean easily. Protect the wall behind easels with a sheet of clear plastic. A drying rack offers a protected

SAFETY FIRST IN THE ART CENTER

There are many art materials that contain dangerous toxins. Under the age of 12, children tend to be more vulnerable to these toxic substances than adults because they're smaller and their growing cells absorb more toxins. Use this list to ensure that your art center is a creative, healthy place for children.

Unsafe Substances for Children:

- Permanent felt-tip markers
OK: Water-based markers

- Powdered tempera paint/pastels that create dust (can cause respiratory problems)
OK: Liquid or pre-mixed paint

- Clay in powder form (can cause silicosis, marked by shortness of breath)
OK: Wet clay

- Instant papier-mâché (may contain asbestos fibers and can cause respiratory illness)
OK: papier-mâché made from old newspaper and paste

- Solvents such as turpentine, benzene, and toluene; and products containing solvents such as rubber cement, epoxy glues, or silk-screening materials (can damage brain and liver)
OK: Water-based materials

- Aerosol spray paint (contains solvents, toxic pigments, and fixatives)
OK: Water-based paints

- Photographic chemicals (can cause anemia)
OK: Blueprint paper

- Leaded glazes (which can cause lead poisoning)
OK: Poster paint (but do not serve food on painted objects)

More questions? Arts, Crafts, and Theater Safety in New York will answer questions by telephone. Call (212) 777-0062 weekdays during regular business hours. Note: This is a toll call outside New York City.

place for paintings to dry. A clothesline strung at children's height in an out-of-the-way corner also works well as a substitute.

■ **Storage Shelves** – Store supplies on low, open shelves to allow for children's easy, independent access. Low shelving units also help to separate the art center from the rest of your room or define spaces for different projects and processes within the area itself. Shelves turned to face out into the rest of the room provide great places to display paintings, drawings, prints, and collages within the art area. Show off clay forms and constructions on top of shelves.

■ **Teacher Storage** – Extra supplies and materials, such as sharp scissors (for adult use only), should not be stored on children's shelves. It's not only potentially dangerous, but it's also confusing to children to have materials close by that they may not touch. Try to place a storage cupboard or closet (with doors) adjacent to your art area for extra supplies and special equipment.

■ **Cleanup Item**s – Organize items in ways that will encourage children to practice the art of cleanup. Hang smocks on low pegs in the area. Keep a large wastebasket in the center for disposing of paper scraps too small or messy to be used again and a basket for recyclable materials. Set out sponges; pans or buckets of soapy water; child-sized mops, brooms, and dustpans; and paper towels for washing hands and cleaning up paint spills, chalk smears, drips, etc.

STOCKING YOUR SUPPLY SHELVES

A lively assortment of materials is critical to a successful art area. However, the age and the experience of your children will determine the number and types of materials you'll want to provide. With twos and young threes, start with very basic materials and put out just a few choices at a time, varying what's offered to maintain interest. As children grow more familiar with different art processes, increase the variety.

Below are guidelines on basic materials. For a wider assortment of materials to use with each of the basic processes, see "Variety Is the Spice of Art!" on pages 28-29.

■ *Paper* – Manila, construction, and white drawing paper; and wallpaper samples. Put out a few sheets of each kind and replenish as needed. Set up a paper-scraps box for leftovers to use for other activities such as collages.

■ *Drawing materials* – Large and small crayons, colored pencils, and markers (water-based only).

■ *Scissors* – Blunt, right-handed and left-handed, or newer types that can be used with either hand; and loop trainers for very young children.

■ *Glue/Paste* – Nontoxic white glue and commercial or homemade paste (see recipe, page 25). Use small containers, such as medicine cups or jar lids, and cotton-tipped swabs or popsicle sticks for spreading.

■ *Tempera and finger paint* – Dry tempera is unsafe for children (see "Safety First in the Art Center," page 23). Pre-mix tempera away from children to a smooth and dripless consistency. Store in large gallon jugs in your cupboard, and give children small amounts, replenishing as needed. Purchase finger paint or make your own (see recipe, page 25).

■ *Paintbrushes* – Short-handled, flat-bristled easel brushes are a must. Soak brushes in soapy water between painters, but be sure to wash and dry them each day, as prolonged soaking loosens the bristles. Enlist children's help.

■ *Modeling materials* – Playdough, plasticene, and potter's earth clay. Provide tools such as scissors, tongue depressors, and popsicle sticks for cutting and shaping.

Playdough is easily malleable and the best choice for younger children, though all ages love it. It has a pleasant fragrance, vibrant color, and a soft, springy texture. Buy it commercially, or make your own (see recipe, page 25).

Baked playdough works best when children want to save their creations.

Plasticene, or "modeling clay," is an oil-based clay that doesn't dry out. It's hard to manipulate when cold, so let it warm up before offering it to children. Plasticene comes in many colors and can be mixed to form new colors. (Recommended for fours and older.)

Earth clay can be purchased in art-supply stores, pre-mixed in 25-pound bags. Store the clay wrapped in plastic in a container with a tight-fitting lid, such as a small garbage pail, to keep it wet. It's messier than other clays so be sure children wear smocks. (Clay in powder form is hazardous to children, but wet clay is safe for them to use. See "Safety First in the Art Center," page 23.)

A PLACE FOR EVERYTHING

A well-organized art area with materials in good condition, stored consistently in the same place, encourages creative, independent, well-disciplined activity. A messy center with dried-up, worn-out materials that are scattered helter-skelter encourages chaos. Granted, it takes planning to set up an organizational system, but the time you spend now will save quite a bit of time later.

Most materials should have their own special container with a designated location on the children's shelves, identified by a picture label, a silhouette of the container, or both. Paper can be stacked directly on a shelf, but it, too, needs a special spot and label. Here are ideas for containers to use for storing or working with various materials.

- **Transparent Plastic Boxes** – These are ideal for storing many types of materials because children can see what's inside. For example, designate a transparent "collage" box and vary the assortment of materials you place in it from week to week.
- **Scissor Homes** – A coffee can with holes in the plastic lid makes a good storage container for children's scissors.

Or cut off the bottom of an egg carton, turn it upside down, and punch a hole in each cup to store a dozen scissors. A brightly colored basket could also be used, and, of course, you can buy scissor racks.

- **Crayon Cans** – Cover clean juice cans with color-coded self-stick paper to hold color-sorted crayons and markers. Place colored circles on the shelf to indicate the special spot for each can.
- **Marker Anchors** – Here's a solution to the lost-caps problem that causes water-based markers to dry out. Pour 1/2 inch of plaster of paris into a shallow container. Sink inverted marker caps into the plaster and let it harden. Markers are stored upside down, and no more lost caps!
- **Collage Collectors** – Rinsed coffee cans and potato chip tubes make great containers for holding sorted collage materials or accessory items to use with modeling or construction materials. Glue a sample of the items stored inside on the cover of each can.
- **Brush Holders** – Use a coffee can or large plastic jar with a wide base to hold clean brushes, bristle-end up.
- **Paint Partners** – To reduce paint spills, cut holes in regular kitchen sponges that are the size of your paint cups. Insert the cups into the sponges to help stabilize them and to absorb drips. These can be used in easel trays or on table tops. Muffin tins make good paint holders for table-top painting. Leave one cup empty and one or two filled with water to encourage color mixing.

Finally, in the place-for-everything category, designate where children can safely and easily place finished products without having to ask permission This prevents collage pieces from fluttering to the floor, a wet painting from smearing a passing peer, or a cardboard-tube sculpture from becoming a Leaning Tower of Pisa look-alike!

TAKING ART OUTDOORS

Outdoors is a wonderful setting for art activities! In fact, it can be a more enjoyable setting than indoors for very

DO-IT-YOURSELF SUPPLIES

One way to lessen the cost of art materials is to make some of the basics. Recipes for homemade paste, playdough, and finger paint abound. Add these to your own favorites.

COOKED PLAYDOUGH

4 cups flour
2 cups salt
4 tablespoons cream of tartar
4 cups water
2 tablespoons vegetable oil
food coloring

Add coloring to water to desired shade. Combine ingredients and cook over medium heat, stirring constantly until stiff. Let cool, then knead. Store in an airtight container. This dough is springy and long-lasting.

CLASSROOM PASTE

1 1/2 cups water
2 tablespoons light corn syrup
1 teaspoon white vinegar
1/2 cup cornstarch
oil of cloves, wintergreen, or other scent (optional)

Combine 3/4 cup water with corn syrup and vinegar in a saucepan. Bring to a boil, then remove from heat. Stir cornstarch into remaining 3/4 cup water until smooth. Slowly add to cooked mixture, stirring constantly until smooth. Add scented oil. Let sit for a day to develop consistency of paste. Store in a covered 2 1/2 cup container (keeps eight weeks).

SUPER SIMPLE FINGER PAINT

liquid starch or liquid dishwashing detergent
dry tempera paint

Slowly mix the dry tempera paint with the starch or dishwashing detergent until you have desired thickness and quantity. This recipe lets you make finger paint as often as you like and only in the amount you need. Vary the colors each time to add interest.

messy activities like spatter and spray-bottle painting, or anytime children really need to spread out, such as when working on group murals. The outdoors is also rich with possibilities for texture rubbings. Giant chalk is even more fun to draw with on sidewalks. Chain-link fences provide a great mesh for weaving. Try setting up your easels outside, and observe how the subjects and even the colors children choose change in a new environment.

As you plan for outdoor art activities, remember that there are some special considerations to keep in mind.

■ **Supervision** – In a new setting, children may work less independently and require more assistance from you. Be sure there are enough adult eyes and ears to help young artists and to observe children who may be otherwise engaged on the playground.

■ **Choice** – Turn outdoor activities into special projects, such as creating a mural or painting on the sidewalk. Vary the activity each time, but don't try to offer children the same range of activities you do inside. Toting the materials

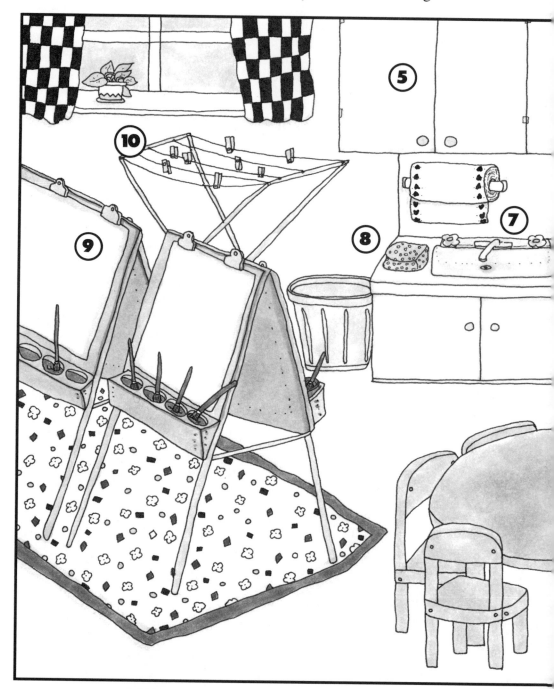

outside and supervising several activities at once will be too difficult. Make outdoor art fun for yourself as well as your children!

■ **Weather** – Before you pack up the paints and head outside, be sure there are no thunderclouds on the horizon. Mild days with little or no wind are good times for outdoor art.

■ **Cleanup** – Bring along a bucket of soapy water and plenty of paper towels for cleaning up outdoors. Don't wait to get inside to wash hands, etc., or you may have a trail of pint-sized finger-prints to clean up later! And besides, cleanup is part of the process — indoors or out.

Despite the logistics, take art outdoors whenever possible, particularly if you have a summer program. It's refreshing for children, especially for those who appreciate the chance to let go with a water bottle and "paint" the sidewalk. And it's one more way to make art creative, exciting, and wonderfully surprising!

Sylvia Tritch is Ohio District Manager of Children's World Learning Centers in Centerville, Ohio.

AN IDEAL SET-UP

The illustration at left shows an art area designed to help children feel free to express themselves in independent and creative ways. The numbers in the illustration coincide with the suggestions below. Please refer to "Setting Up Your Art Center," pages 22-29, for more detailed guidelines.

1. Set up your art shelf using labels. Store items on low shelves to help children feel independent and to help you stay organized.

2. Hang smocks or oilcloth aprons on low hooks where children can reach them.

3. If possible, provide a special table for children to use when they are working with clay.

4. Provide at least one table where children can work on art projects together or independently.

5. Use higher, closed shelves to store items you'd rather not have children use or that require close adult supervision.

6. Make sure you have plenty of bulletin boards to display children's work.

7. If possible, provide a sink (or water source) so children can wash their hands, help clean up, and add water to their art work.

8. Provide large waste baskets, paper towels, and sponges so children can help clean up.

9. Provide easels, paints, and a washable drop cloth.

10. Help children learn to use drying racks and clothespins so their paintings can dry completely, out of harm's way.

VARIETY IS THE SPICE OF ART!

Variety is the watchword when gathering art materials for young children. To help inspire your own creativity, refer to this list for ideas. You'll find many of the materials are simple odds and ends that can be used with several processes. They're also listed with ages and stages in mind. More basic materials are suggested for the youngest children, with more options added for older ones who have more experience with each process. Remember, older children will still enjoy most of the supplies and many of the activities listed for younger ones.

Don't worry about giving children ideas on what to do with specific materials. When they're first exposed to new art materials, children tend to explore them just as they do with anything new, testing them for limits and possibilities.

DRAWING

OBJECTS TO DRAW WITH
- **Twos** – Fat and thin crayons; and wide, water-based markers
- **Threes** – Thick, soft-lead pencils; colored pencils; and cotton swabs dipped in paint
- **Fours** – Narrow-tipped water-based markers and dustless colored chalk
- **Fives** – Ball-point pens, charcoal sticks, and grease pencils

MATERIALS TO DRAW ON
- **Twos** – Colored paper, old stationery, newsprint, computer paper, typing paper, shelf paper, paper plates, and concrete (sidewalk)
- **Threes** – Bumpy watercolor paper, sandpaper, wallpaper samples, cardboard, shoebox lids, grocery sacks, and lunch bags
- **Fours** – Adding-machine rolls, drawing paper, small note pads, and faces (with washable makeup pencils)
- **Fives** – Index cards, tracing paper, unpainted wood scraps, acetate report covers (use grease pencils), and old slides (Adults clean slides using cotton dipped in chlorine bleach; children use grease pencils to create new pictures to project!)

PAINTING

THINGS TO USE AS PAINT
- **Twos and Threes** – Liquid tempera, finger paint, plain or colored water, and shaving cream
- **Fours and Fives** – Watercolor in trays; oil paints or acrylics in tubes, squeezed on a pallet (supervise closely); and latex house paint (on wood outside)
- **For Experienced Painters** – Change the consistency of tempera paints from time to time. Add more water to make thin, runny paint or more paint for a thick, gloppy substance. Mix in other materials to change the quality or texture, such as coffee grounds, cornstarch, flour, glycerine, liquid detergent, starch, sand, and sawdust.

OBJECTS TO PAINT WITH
- **Twos** – Short-handled brushes about 1/2 inch in width, housepainting brushes of different widths (for painting with water outside), fingers and hands, and sponges (attach spring-type clothespins as handles)
- **Threes** – Easel brushes, toothbrushes, cotton-tipped swabs, and sponge pompoms
- **Fours** – Scrub brushes, combs, bare feet, ice cubes, paint rollers, pine-needle boughs, and spray bottles
- **Fives** – Soft- and hard-bristled artists' brushes of various widths

SURFACES TO PAINT ON
- **Twos and Threes** – Manila, shelf, and construction paper; old file folders; large and small paper sacks; rocks; boxes; and corrugated cardboard
- **Fours and Fives** – Aluminum foil, mural and waxed paper, and windows

PRINT-MAKING
OBJECTS TO PRINT WITH
- **Twos and Threes** – Hands and feet, plastic cookie cutters, jar lids, potato mashers and other safe kitchen gadgets, rubber blocks, sponges, spools, and raw vegetables and fruits
- **Fours and Fives** – Burlap or onion bags glued to cardboard, corrugated cardboard, keys, pot scrubbers, rubber erasers, puzzle pieces, commercial rubber stamps, sneaker soles, plastic fruit baskets, toothpicks glued in a design on cardboard, and textured hair rollers

MATERIALS TO PRINT ON

- **Twos and Threes** – Construction paper, grocery sacks, mural paper, newsprint, and shelf paper
- **Fours and Fives** – Aluminum foil or shiny wrapping paper, bumpy watercolor paper, and unlined index cards

PRINTING TECHNIQUES

- **Finger Prints** – Offer children opportunities to finger-paint directly on a tabletop. To add interest, sprinkle glitter, salt, or sand on the paint before making a print. Children can place newsprint over the paint, press carefully so paper doesn't slide around, then pick up one corner (assist as needed) to lift off the paper, revealing the reversed print.
- **Tray Prints** – Give each child a clean plastic foam meat tray. The child uses a blunt pencil or popsicle stick to draw a design on the bottom of the tray. Cover the design with tempera paint, then with a sheet of paper. Press lightly to make a print.
- **Glue Prints** – Give each child heavy cardboard and white glue in a squeeze bottle. The child creates the design on cardboard with glue. Let the glue dry, cover with paint, and then with paper to make a print. Or invert the glue design onto a homemade paint pad (see below) to use as a stamp.
- **Bubble Prints** – Place about an inch of water in a small bowl or margarine tub. Add a generous amount of food coloring and a squirt of liquid detergent. Using a straw, ask a child to blow a froth of bubbles that comes up over the top of the container. Then help the child carefully place white construction paper over the container and lift up to reveal a circular print of bubble marks. Offer bowls with different colors, and encourage children to overlap prints for interesting effects.
- **Do-It-Yourself Stamp Pad** – Place a sponge or sponge cloth in a clean plastic foam grocery tray. Pour liquid tempera onto the sponge or cloth until it's soaked with paint. Use this like an ink pad, adding more paint as needed. Cover when not in use to keep sponge from drying out.
- **Clay Stamps** – Give each child plasticene to shape into a flat pancake. Encourage the child to use a blunt pencil to draw a design in the clay and cover the design with tempera paint. Invert clay "stamp" onto clean paper, press lightly, then lift off to reveal the print. Since plasticene is oil-based, the paint can be washed off and the "stamp" used again.
- **Shoe-Liner Stamps** – Give each child a foam-rubber shoe liner to draw shapes on. Cut out the shapes, then glue onto a small block of wood to use as a printing stamp.

COLLAGE AND CONSTRUCTION

STICKY MATERIALS

- **Twos and Threes** – Homemade and commercial paste, non-toxic white glue, and masking tape
- **Fours and Fives** – Nontoxic glue sticks; transparent, cellophane, colored, fabric, and electrical tapes; and self-stick paper

MATERIALS TO GET "STUCK" ON

- **Twos and Threes** – Construction paper; cellophane; corrugated cardboard; aluminum foil; tissue paper; fabrics such as cotton, wool, velour, corduroy, felt, leather, lace, fake fur, and burlap; yarn; ribbon; thread; and rickrack
- **Fours and Fives** – Buttons, beads, and old jewelry; natural items such as weeds, pinecones, seeds, shells, sand, wood curls, bark, and leaves; bottle caps; corks; cotton balls; toothpicks; small paper cups; cupcake papers; plastic foam packing pieces; paper doilies; straws; string or twine; and gummed labels and stars

SURFACES TO CREATE ON

- construction paper (for paper and fabric collages)
- cut-up grocery boxes
- egg cartons
- grocery sacks and lunch bags
- grocery trays (cardboard and foam)
- paper plates
- old file folders
- shoeboxes or shoebox lids
- wood scraps

MATERIALS TO BUILD WITH

- flat, smooth pieces of wood or cardboard (to use as the base for construction)
- boxes of all sizes — from soap boxes to large cartons (also good bases)
- empty tubes from wrapping paper, paper towels, toilet tissue, etc.
- empty thread spools
- plastic foam packing pieces (peanuts, cubes, rings, saucers, etc.)
- odd pieces from manipulative sets

MODELING

MATERIALS TO USE WITH CLAY, PLASTICENE, OR PLAYDOUGH

When children have had plenty of experience with modeling materials alone, offer accessory materials they can use to create impressions in the clay or decorate their shapes, such as the following:

- **Twos and Threes** – Combs, cookie cutters, jar lids, keys, plastic building toys, plastic hair curlers, shells, and empty thread and tape spools
- **Fours and Fives** – Bottle caps; coins; garlic presses; old jewelry; plastic letters and numbers; rubber stamps; and screws, nuts, bolts, and washers

EXTENDING ART TO CHILDREN WITH SPECIAL NEEDS

Creative art activities can be especially enriching for special-needs children, who often require additional support in the areas of physical, cognitive, social, and emotional development. The benefits of art in these areas are clear. Creative art experiences help to increase self-esteem, self-confidence, and attention span; enhance cognitive and fine-motor skills; and provide a meaningful setting for learning to share space, materials, and cleanup chores. And for a child who may often feel anger and frustration because of a handicapping condition, creative art experiences offer an acceptable outlet for expressing emotions.

WORKING WITH SPECIAL-NEEDS CHILDREN IN THE ART AREA

Generally, the way you approach art with special-needs children is the same as with any other child.

■ *Emphasize process over product.* Encourage each child to feel free to explore materials and techniques. Remember, the same rules for responding to and respecting children's artwork apply to special-needs children. As you know, it is a frustrating experience for children to try to meet an adult's expectation of a painted flower or a molded dish. It is even more so for a special-needs child.

■ *Look for ways to accommodate a range of skill levels.* For example, two children are busy cutting and pasting paper to make collages. A child with special needs who has not mastered cutting with a scissors wants to join in.

Consider sitting with the child and quietly demonstrating how to tear off pieces of paper in free-form shapes to glue onto paper. The intriguing look of the torn pieces may even encourage other children to try this method. But more importantly, you've helped the special-needs child to feel a part of the group while functioning on the level at which he or she can experience success.

The guidelines that follow offer general tips and suggestions to ensure more successful art experiences for children with particular needs. You'll also want to consult parents and therapists for specific ideas on how to work with individual children in your group.

HEARING-IMPAIRED CHILDREN

Because the act of creating is nonverbal, art can be deeply satisfying for children with hearing impairments. Listening and speaking are needed primarily for getting instructions and materials or for talking about the artwork. Overall, children with a hearing loss can function quite normally in the art area, and this can be the source of enhanced confidence and self-esteem!

TIPS AND REMINDERS:
■ Be sure you have children's attention before giving instructions. Look directly into their faces, and speak clearly at a normal speed and volume.
■ As needed, provide hearing-impaired children with visual cues for rules, instructions, or techniques. For example, you might draw pictures of the steps in making a print, or demonstrate the process.

VISUALLY IMPAIRED CHILDREN

Many art activities are very tactile. Visually impaired children can have great fun and benefit, too, from manipulating clay or playdough, then feeling the results. Depending on the degree of sight loss, there are ways to improve your physical environment so that visually impaired children can take part in a broader range of activities.

TIPS AND REMINDERS:

■ Take visually impaired children on a tour of the art area to help them learn the location of tables, easels, paper, paints, clay, etc. If you rearrange the area at any time, be sure to reorient children. Remind others not to place artworks-in-progress or materials in walking paths or workplaces.

■ Provide extra light in the art area for children who have some useful vision. Make sure the light is evenly distributed and not glaring.

■ Set up children who have some vision at easels or drafting tables that can be positioned at an angle. This way children can comfortably hold their faces close to the work surface when they need to.

■ Find out which colors each visually impaired child sees best, then supply materials in those hues.

■ When introducing new materials, give visually impaired children extra time to touch and explore them.

CHILDREN WITH PHYSICAL IMPAIRMENTS

Children with physical disabilities often have special difficulties in the art area. Depending on the particular condition, they may have trouble holding tools, controlling movements, or maneuvering wheelchairs and other aids around the tight spaces of the area. To fully involve physically impaired children in art activities, you may need to rearrange your setting to meet particular needs. However, the reorganizing is worth the effort when it helps every

child feel a part of the group.

TIPS AND REMINDERS:

■ For children with orthopedic handicaps, the best position for doing art activities is on the floor, with a bolster under the chest. This allows for optimum shoulder and arm movement. As much as possible, try to involve the children in floor-based art activities, such as working on a group mural or box sculpture.

■ So children in wheelchairs can work comfortably at tables, be sure the wheelchair arms fit easily under the furniture. If the tables aren't high enough, raise the level by nailing blocks of wood securely under the legs.

■ If a child can sit supported, use straps to secure him or her to a chair. Remember, the child should be well balanced and able to move his shoulders and arms freely. If the child is prone to involuntary movements, allow plenty of space between him and others so there's no danger of those movements splattering paint on others or bumping another child's artwork.

■ Tape paper to the table or floor so that it remains secure as the child paints, draws, or glues on it.

■ Offer paste in wide-mouth jars and glue in squeeze bottles.

■ If children cannot easily hold an art tool, wrap tape around it to expand the width. Or cut a slit in a small rubber ball, insert the tool, and have the child hold the ball to manipulate the tool.

MENTALLY RETARDED CHILDREN

The key to helping mentally retarded children feel successful in the art area is guiding them toward activities that are appropriate for their developmental age. For example, a three-year-old functioning at two-year-old level will work best with simple materials such as large crayons and easel paints. For other levels, try these materials or activities:

■ 2 1/2 – 3 1/2 years: Colored pencils, water-based markers, liquid tempera paints and brushes in various sizes,

SPECIAL TIPS FOR SPECIAL CHILDREN

Because of their particular handicaps, art activities are often most challenging for visually and physically impaired children. Here you'll find activity and project ideas, as well as ideas on how to help any child with that "bugaboo" skill — learning to cut!

TEXTURE AND DIMENSION FOR THE VISUALLY IMPAIRED

◆ Add sawdust, sand, or glitter to paint so that the child can feel what he or she has painted.

◆ Provide paper with lots of texture for painting or drawing, such as corrugated cardboard and wallpaper.

◆ Offer beads, yarn, buttons, packing pieces, and other objects with dimension for gluing onto paper.

◆ Tape a mesh screen to drawing paper. As the child draws on the paper with crayon, the screen creates a wax imprint the child can feel.

◆ Provide felt, buttons, string, yarn, and rubber bands for making raised features on paper-bag puppets.

TOUCH AND FEEL FOR THE PHYSICALLY IMPAIRED

Many children with physical impairments are sensitive to touch and need encouragement to work with paste and other highly tactile materials. Provide items with varied textures, such as burlap, felt, and sandpaper, to use in a collage. But also give children time to get used to the way these materials feel.

◆ Sculpting with clay or playdough helps improve fine-motor strength and skill. Start with playdough, which is easier to work with than clay. If necessary, soften the playdough by warming and kneading it. Give physically impaired children a surface that's hard, smooth, and stable to work on.

◆ Let children finger-paint directly on a table surface. Encourage them to use their fists, palms, fingers — whatever parts they can control most easily.

SCISSORS SUCCESS FOR EVERY CHILD!

Look for special scissors designed with two sets of holes. Your fingers go in one set, while the child's go in the other, allowing you to manipulate the scissors with the child and to gradually relinquish control. Start by giving the child playdough and having him or her snip off short pieces. Progress to paper, letting him cut freely at first. When the child is ready to tackle lines, draw straight or slightly curved lines for him to follow. For a visually impaired child, use glue to create raised lines for the child to follow. The child feels the dried glue with one hand as he cuts along the lines with scissors.

paper of different sizes and textures, finger paints, clay, and playdough

■ 3 1/2 – 4 1/2 years: Watercolors, dustless chalk, papier-mâché, collage materials, sand-casting, print-making, and "junk" sculptures

It is important to remember that mentally retarded children progress through developmental stages more slowly than their same-age peers. They require more adult guidance to learn to use materials and more time to work with them. When classmates are ready to try a new art activity, the mentally retarded peer may still be repeating a familiar activity. While you want the mentally retarded child to experience success, once he masters a tool or technique help him enhance skills by trying new challenges. Be patient and persistent, even if the child initially resists.

TIPS AND REMINDERS:

■ Limit the number of materials available to the child at one time. Too many choices can be overwhelming.

■ To encourage a child to experiment with art tools, make suggestions or model ideas. You might say to the child, "Kyle, try pressing hard with your crayon like I'm doing. Now make a soft line like this. See the difference in how the lines and the colors look?"

■ Remember, mentally retarded children often have trouble making transitions. Warn the child five minutes in advance that cleanup time is approaching, and issue reminders every few minutes. Assign him a cleanup job, such as washing his paintbrush and hands.

CHILDREN WITH BEHAVIOR DISTURBANCES

These children may commonly display one of three types of extreme behaviors: hyperactivity, aggression, or withdrawal. Art activities can be therapeutic — calming, and helping to increase attention spans, social skills, and self-images.

Remember, children with behavior problems often need more adult guidance with art activities. That doesn't mean telling the child what to create. Rather, it means helping the child organize the steps he or she wants to take in creating. For example, if a child is making a collage, you might suggest that she first tear paper into strips; next, cut pieces of yarn she's chosen; and last, paste the items on paper in a way she likes.

TIPS AND REMINDERS:

■ Messy materials can disturb or overexcite children with behavior disturbances, leading to behavior extremes. Steer them toward choices like crayons and playdough.

■ Offer a limited number of materials. Too much stimulation makes it harder for a hyperactive or aggressive child to control behavior.

■ Allow a withdrawn child to watch others. This is so the child can become familiar with an art activity before trying it.

■ Put your arm around the shoulders of a hyperactive child as she works. Direct the child verbally to keep her attention on the activity. You might say, "Sally, what color clay would you like? See if you can roll it between your hands." Encourage the child to work independently, but if she loses interest, suggest new ideas to refocus attention: "You made a snake with clay. It's so long! Now what else would you like to make? How about a ball or a fish?"

■ Be liberal with your praise. Comment positively when a child stays with a project, works with others, or shares materials.

■ As cleanup time approaches, inform children in advance. Children with behavior problems also have trouble with transitions. Repeat your reminders every few minutes. Assign children specific tasks to do.

Merle Karnes, Ed.D., is a professor of special education at the University of Illinois at Urbana.

TALKING WITH FAMILIES ABOUT CREATIVE ART

You know that for art to be a real source of discovery, creativity, and enhanced self-esteem for children, the people who are most important in their lives must understand and support the goals and benefits of a creative art program. As you talk with parents and other family members, remember that many adults' own childhood experiences cause them to focus on products when they think about art. And when children bring something home, parents and family members may not understand that those wild splotches of color are far more exciting and rewarding for the child than a color-in-the-lines page could ever be. Your challenge is to help families understand the value of creative art in every aspect of their child's development. These ideas can help.

■ *Communicate*. First and foremost, share your philosophy. Make art a discussion point during parent meetings right from the beginning. Explain how a child's developmental level influences his or her creation. Help them recognize the joy, pride, and sense of discovery and wonder their children feel when engaged in a creative activity. Catch the "teachable moments" to educate families about children and art.

■ *Solve the easily solved problems.* Evaluate the concerns families express. You may find some problems are more practical than philosophical. For instance, a parent may be reluctant to encourage "messy" activities because his or her child came home with a paint-smeared shirt. Make sure everyone has old clothes to wear for art. Another parent may be feeling that her child, who is much more interested in

process, brings no artwork home. Make an effort to roll a few paintings up to send home, "just for Mom and Dad to enjoy, too."

■ *Share the joy.* Family members often miss seeing their child's pleasure in doing art, so look for ways to share that joy. Take instant photos of children at work, record comments as a child creates, invite a child to dictate a story about a work-in-progress, or make sure you share a particular incident at pickup time.

■ *Let families in on the fun.* A family-night workshop can help parents understand the fun and excitement of creative art. Present materials as you would to children, letting adults choose what they would like to work with and giving them plenty of time to create. Point out skills they're demonstrating that children practice, too — decision-making, problem-solving, language, fine-motor, etc. Also use this gathering to educate families on how to encourage creative expression. For example, you might hold up a painting by van Gogh or Monet, or a picture of a sculpture by Rodin or Michelangelo. Invite adults to create copies of these masterpieces and, when the laughter subsides, help them connect their own feelings of inadequacy and creative repression to those of children when presented with adult-made models.

■ *Send home reminders.* Copy the sheet on the following page, as well as any of the pages noted on page 2, to help support your philosophy that creative art contributes to an exciting foundation for future growth!

LEARNING THROUGH CREATIVE ART:
A MESSAGE TO FAMILIES

Dear Parents,

Take a peek at our art center on any given day to watch your child and others as they use art materials in their own unique ways. The kinds of activities you'll observe represent our belief that young children create more expressively when they're free to enjoy the process of creating, rather than instructed to make a product that an adult has chosen or is directing. We give children interesting materials and a comfortable place where they can work, and let the ideas come from their own creative selves.

As the most important person in your child's life, you can help to encourage his or her creativity. Here are ways to support your child's self-expression through art.

▪ What do you say to a scribble?

Sometimes it's hard to know how to comment on an abstract scribble. Avoid asking, "What is this supposed to be?" Instead, recognize that your child may have enjoyed experimenting with materials with no theme in mind. Statements that describe what you see — "Looks like you had fun with purple today!" — let your child know you're really looking at the picture, but not judging it.

▪ The art gallery is open!

Displaying your child's artwork also says that you value his or her creative efforts. The refrigerator may be your favorite place. Or find an old picture frame, cut a paper mat to fit, and make this a place of honor for paintings, drawings, and collages.

▪ Help yourself to the art shelf.

When your child engages in creative art, many important skills are enhanced: fine-motor and eye-hand coordination, language, and creative-thinking and problem-solving skills, to name just a few. Build on those skills by setting up your own art center at home. Designate an accessible shelf on which to keep materials. Label containers for storing such items as child-safe scissors, crayons, water-based markers, colored pencils, different kinds of tape, and nontoxic glue. Add materials to draw on or to cut out and glue, such as typing paper, old greeting cards, and scraps of fabric, ribbon, and gift wrap.

▪ The family that finger-paints together ...

From time to time, try a special activity together, such as making finger paint. Dissolve 1/2 cup cornstarch in 1 cup cold water, then pour into 3 cups boiling water. Stir constantly until shiny and translucent. Cool, then color with food dye. (You can also mix in sand to give the paint a gritty texture or a tablespoon of glycerin to make it slick and smooth.) Cover a table with paper, and enjoy this wonderfully sensory experience together. Invite the whole family to join in the fun!

ACTIVITY PLANS

FOR TWOS, THREES, FOURS, AND FIVES

USING THE ACTIVITY PLANS

Stimulating materials, a comfortable space to create, and the freedom to explore materials and techniques in their own ways are just about all young children need to find joy, wonder, pride, and deep satisfaction in creative art.

But, once in a while, children do need something else you can provide — a spark to recharge their creative energies.

The 40 child-centered plans that follow, designed for children ages two to five, are meant to do just that — suggest new ways to use familiar materials and equipment; introduce children to new techniques; and integrate art into explorations of weather, seasonal change, and other events in children's everyday lives.

These activities are not intended to replace children's own creative play. Rather, they're designed to enhance it, with themes and ideas that are appropriate to the developmental abilities and interests of twos, threes, fours, and fives.

UNDERSTANDING YOUR ROLE

You may be accustomed to thinking of yourself as an observer and assistant in the art area — watching as children select materials and use them in their own expressive ways, refilling the paint cups as needed, and finding a safe spot for a painting when the drying rack is full. The idea of using "activity plans" may sound dangerously like telling children how or what to create.

Rest assured, you won't be. As you use the activity plans your role will still be to inspire children's creativity, enhance their curiosity about various materials and effects, and offer them hands-on learning experiences. The plans are child-centered and designed to encourage open-ended exploration. When might you use an activity plan? Perhaps you notice that the easels are getting "old" and children are painting less frequently. Try a plan that offers a novel easel-related activity. Pull out a plan for an outdoor activity on a sunny summer day. Introduce a new technique when you think children are ready for something different. You know when children are growing restless with the familiar. That's the time to flip through these activity plans.

You'll find that the plans require a minimum of your direct involvement. Once you've introduced an activity, you can step back and let the children experiment and discover, solve problems, and make decisions — all on their own. You can look for appropriate times to comment and ask questions, and assist when you're really needed. But you'll find you're just as much of an observer and assistant with an activity plan as without, because you're giving children time and space to make their own discoveries, while insuring that their art experiences are rich, rewarding — and fun!

GETTING THE MOST FROM THE ACTIVITY PLANS

While the plans have been written and designed for children ages two to five, these ages represent a wide range of developmental levels. You may find that certain plans need to be adapted to meet the particular needs and interests of your group. The key is to be aware of your children's developmental levels and to look for ways to enhance their interests and experiences with appropriate activities.

The format is simple and easy to follow. Each plan includes most of these sections:

- **Aim:** The value of the activity is outlined through a listing of the learning and developmental areas that will be tapped.

- **Group Size:** The suggested group size is the optimum number of children to involve at one time. Naturally, you can adjust this number to meet your needs.

- **Materials:** Basic art materials or special items to gather are suggested here. As well, ingredients for making materials, such as homemade playdough, may also be listed.

- **In Advance:** This is an occasional heading found in some plans. It often suggests materials to make or to gather before introducing the activity to children.

- **Getting Ready:** Here you'll find suggested ways to introduce the theme to a large group at circle time or to a small group. Open-ended questions help children think about a topic. Brainstorming ideas, creating experience charts, taking a nature walk to observe or gather materials, or reading recommended stories are other ways to encourage involvement.

- **Begin:** This is where the real creating begins! Suggestions for introducing the materials and for helping children get

started are included with each plan. There are also open-ended questions that will stimulate children to seek other ways to use a material or to test a technique. Some activities also feature variations or extension ideas to further enhance an experience.

- **Remember:** This section offers developmental considerations to keep in mind when planning the activity, safety tips, and suggested ways to expand an activity or relate other skills and concepts, such as story writing.

- **Books:** The books listed at the bottom of each page have been carefully selected to reinforce the art-activity theme. They can be read before the activity to build interest, or after, to follow up the enjoyment.

SHARING THE PLANS WITH OTHERS

To get the most from the activity plans featured in this guide, make them available to assistant teachers, aides, volunteers, and family members. (You have permission to duplicate all activity pages for educational use.)

When you share these plans, you communicate your philosophy of child-centered learning to others. By offering tips on how to plan, organize, and present art activities, you help other adults to understand the vast and exciting potential of art experiences to express children's ideas, feelings, and startling imaginations!

USING THE ACTIVITY INDEX

The index on pages 78-79 lists each activity plan, along with the developmental areas and skills it enhances. Use the index to:

- determine the full range of skills and concepts covered in the plans

- highlight specific skills a plan reenforces when talking with family members

- see which activities have the potential to encourage social skills, such as casual interaction or cooperation and sharing

- identify and locate an activity that reinforces particular creative or cognitive skills on which you want to focus

- assist you in finding activities that complement your group's present interests

ART

Have fun collecting natural items and using them to create works of art.

STICKY THINGS

Aim: Children will experience a feeling of independence and develop an awareness of their natural surroundings while using gross- and fine-motor skills.

Group size: Three or four children.

Materials: Small paper bags; crayons; markers; stickers; clear vinyl adhesive; and natural items such as leaves, acorns, pinecones, small rocks and stones, and tall and short grasses.

In Advance: As children arrive, offer each a small paper bag and suggest that the child decorate the bag using crayons, markers, and stickers. Explain that later you will go outside together to collect special things to put in the bags. When children are finished decorating, mark each bag with the child's initials or name and put aside. Choose an area outside where toddlers will be able to find natural items safely and easily.

GETTING READY

Take children outside, and sit together in a quiet place. Talk about what you will do — look for interesting and special things to put in your bags, such as leaves, pinecones, grass, acorns, small rocks, etc. Then hand children their bags and help them search. Supervise carefully to steer them away from litter. End the search as children lose interest.

BEGIN

Back inside, invite children to spread out their natural treasures to observe what they found. Use descriptive language to discuss the items: "Look, Lillian has a beautiful red leaf." "Tommy found a rock that sparkles." "Let's feel April's long, brown grass."

Place a piece of clear vinyl adhesive, sticky side up, in front of you. Invite children to feel its sticky surface. Encourage them to experiment by putting an item on the sticky part of the paper, then turning the paper upside down. Does the item stick? Do any of the items fall off?

Give individual pieces of vinyl adhesive to children who want to make their own collages, and help them peel off the backing. Explain that they can stick as many items on their paper as they like. As children finish, display their work and take time to comment on and to enjoy the variety of textures and colors.

Remember

• Offer art activities throughout the day so that twos can choose when they want to participate.

• Make sure you offer children activities and materials that encourage experimentation. Remember, the experience is more important than the product.

BOOKS

Share with children these simple books about outside things.

• *Ants Go Marching* by Berniece Freschet (Charles Scribner's Sons)

• *Green Eyes* by A. Birnbaum (Golden Press)

• *Sounds My Feet Make* by Arlene Blanchard (Random House)

ART

Pasting is a favorite activity of toddlers. These ideas will keep sticky fingers busy all year long!

FUN WITH PASTE AND GLUE

Aim: Children will enjoy sensory experiences and develop self-expression as they paste materials onto paper.

Group size: One or two children.

Materials: A small or medium-sized box, such as a cigar box or shoebox, covered with washable self-stick paper; bits of torn paper, pictures from magazines, different textures of fabric, cotton balls, and other objects for pasting to go inside the box; paper; and paste or glue.

GETTING READY

Decide ahead of time which materials you will have children paste. Place a few at a time in the pasting box. Fill a container with paste or glue. Place it in the box.

BEGIN

Give each child a piece of paper. Demonstrate how to put paste or glue on the paper by using a small brush or a finger. Now show children the pasting box, and allow them to choose materials from the box to cover as much (or as little) of the paper as they wish. Keep in mind that the process of pasting and discovery is more important to the children than the finished product. Provide oppor-

tunities for twos to describe what they're doing or how things feel as they work: "Sharon, you picked a cotton ball. How does it feel? Is it soft?"

To extend the activity, fill the pasting box with new items throughout the year. You might choose different themes such as pictures of animals, people, vehicles, flowers, etc.

SAND, GLUE, AND TODDLERS, TOO

Aim: Children will have a different gluing experience as they shake sand onto glue designs.

Group size: One or two children.

Materials: Paper, glue, popsicle sticks, fine sand, and sand shakers (see below); and a smock for each child.

In Advance: Make sand shakers by gathering several empty, clean frozen-juice containers with lids. (Be sure to save lids after opening the cans.) Poke several small holes in each lid. Add sand to the containers, and secure the lids in place with heavy tape. Children can use them like salt shakers.

BEGIN

Cover the work area with newspaper. Give each child a large piece of paper. Let children use popsicle sticks to spread glue over their papers. Encourage them to experiment by dripping the glue on their papers, too. Then give them the shakers and watch them shake, shake, shake — sprinkling sand wherever they see glue!

Remember

▪ Twos may glue and reglue the same item while discovering the properties of glue. Don't discourage this kind of repetition. It's one way that twos learn.

▪ Provide twos with opportunities to collect their own items to put into the glue box. Nature walks are good times for collecting objects.

▪ Use real objects as well as pictures for gluing. Leaves, ribbons, plastic foam pieces, plastic lids, and foil pieces are all possibilities. Supervise to ensure twos do not put the objects in their mouths.

▪ Gluing can be done on surfaces other than paper. Try using cardboard or heavy fabric for an interesting change.

BOOKS			
Clean off those sticky fingers and settle down with these stories.	▪ *I Touch* by Helen Oxenbury (Walker)	▪ *Pat the Bunny* by Dorothy Kunhardt (Western)	▪ *Sticky Stanley* by Thomas Crawford (Troll)

ART

Twos love exploring everything ... and sand is no exception!

SAND, SAND, SAND

Aim: Twos will explore the characteristics of wet and dry through several activities.

Group size: One to three children.

Materials: Deep tray filled with sand (one per child); sand toys such as cups, bowls, spoons, funnels, plastic sifters, shovels, and buckets; plastic cookie cutters and other interesting molds; paper cups; water; and dishpans.

GETTING READY

Cover a table with newspaper. For each child, place a tray filled with sand on the table. Place cups filled with water — one for each child — in the middle of the table. (Create a setup for yourself as well.) At the sand table, be sure there are various toys for dumping, filling, pouring, and scooping sand.

BEGIN

SAND PLAY

Invite some children to the sand table. Encourage them to play freely with the toys in the sand. You might add one or two new toys for them to explore with as they play. Provide opportunities for children to talk about what they are doing. Occasionally, verbalize their actions for them: "Jason, I see the sand coming out of

the hole and falling back into the sandbox. Is it falling quickly or slowly?" Encourage children to talk about how the sand feels.

DRAWING IN SAND

For a different activity, seat children at the table and pass out the trays of sand. Demonstrate how to make designs in sand by running your fingers through the sand in your tray. The children will follow your lead. Talk about what each child is doing: "Allie, you made a squiggly line in the sand. Can you make a handprint?" Encourage children to use one finger, two fingers, palms, a spoon, or other instruments to make designs.

WET SAND ART

Take a cup of water and slowly pour it into your tray of sand. Encourage twos to do the same with their water cup and sand pan. As the texture changes, talk about what's happening: "Rico, the sand is sticking together. It must be wet." As children start playing with the wet sand, encourage them to describe how it feels. Mushy? Cold?

SAND MOLDS

Set out a variety of objects that children can use for making molded forms in wet sand, such as plastic cookie cutters in various shapes, cups, bowls, etc. Encourage twos to experiment to see how they can use these objects to make interesting shapes in their pans of wet sand. You may want to play parallel, using your own pan of sand to demonstrate making sand molds. Comment as children make discoveries: "Look, Carmen, you made a star shape in your sand. What kind of shape do you think this cup will make?"

Remember

- Some twos don't like to get their hands dirty. Poking, pushing, scooping, and digging in sand can be accomplished with the sand toys, as well as with straws, blocks, and spoons — and hands will stay clean!
- Some twos will concentrate on the water and will seem uninterested in the sand. Be patient and allow ample time for water exploration. When their interest is "quenched," children should be ready to focus on the sand. Talk about the differences in sand and water.
- Sand can be saved and used several times. Leave it exposed to the air on top of a tall cabinet and let dry. Be sure to keep the sand out of the reach of twos.
- This is a great activity to take outdoors on a warm day.

BOOKS

| Share these books "filled" with sand. | ■ *Beach Day* by Helen Oxenbury (Dial Books) | ■ *Nibble, Nibble* by Margaret Wise Brown (Addison-Wesley) | ■ *The Seashore Noisy Book* by Margaret Wise Brown (Harper & Row) |

ART

Your twos will have fun with this sticky activity!

A TAPE-AND-STICK MURAL

Aim: Children will experiment with the properties of tape while working together to create a mural.

Group size: Whole group.

Materials: Cellophane tape; masking tape; a large piece of butcher-block paper (for mural); scrap and collage materials; various pieces of textured fabrics; and stickers or stamps.

In Advance: Cut strips of masking tape and cellophane tape with which children can experiment. Hang a large piece of butcher paper on the wall, at children's height, for the class "tape mural." Also cut strips of tape to be used on the mural. Partially attach them to the wall or to the bottom of the mural paper so twos can easily take a piece when they want one.

GETTING READY

Introduce the masking and cellophane tapes to children. Demonstrate how a piece of tape can stick to various items you have gathered from around the room. Now let children try sticking the tape to the items you've collected. As they experiment, help them verbalize what is happening: "Sara, I see your piece of tape is sticking to the chair." "Lenny, your tape is sticking to the table." Then gather twos together and talk about what stuck to the tape and what didn't. Were they able to "pick up" any items with the tape?

BEGIN

When children are familiar with tape and its sticky quality, introduce the butcher-block paper and the collage and scrap materials. Invite twos to stick whatever they choose on the mural. As children work (you may need to assist them with the tape), talk about what they are doing: "Reena, that velvet is so soft and smooth. Can you stick it on the paper with the tape?" You might also want to provide stickers for twos to feel and touch, and, of course, to stick on the mural.

Remember

- Twos can use tape to identify body parts. For example, ask, "Can you put tape on your knee? Nose? Elbow?"
- Twos will enjoy using tape to decorate their shoes. Provide different colors, and let the children choose the colors they want to apply. After decorating, have a shoe parade, marching to the playground or just down the hall or around the room.
- Give the mural a theme. For example, for a "blue" mural use blue paper, blue tape, and blue items. Leave it up and add more blue objects daily. Encourage twos to experiment with objects of different sizes, shapes, and weights. Can they tape a blue block or a blue baby blanket to the mural? Talk about why some objects won't stay on the mural.

BOOKS

Help twos discover more about the world of touch with these books.

- *Find Out by Touching* by Paul Showers (Thomas Y. Crowell)

- *Fingers Are Always Bringing Me News* by Mary O'Neil (Doubleday)

- *I Touch* by Helen Oxenbury (Walker)

ART

Let twos "mess around" with finger paint they make themselves.

FINGER-PAINT FUN

Aim: Children will practice observation and fine-motor skills, use their sense of touch, and follow directions as they create and experiment with finger paints.

Group size: Two or three children.

Materials: Measuring cup, mixing bowls, aprons, spoon, white mural paper, and tape; and flour, water, and food coloring for making finger paint.

In Advance: Cover the surface of a table with mural paper and secure with tape. Place all materials on or by the table.

GETTING READY

Gather children around the table. Explain that today they will be finger-painting with special finger paint they make themselves!

Introduce the finger-paint ingredients. Invite children to feel the flour and water. Make the finger paint by measuring 2 cups of flour and 1/4 cup of water. Let children pour the ingredients into the bowl and stir the mixture until it's the thickness of white glue (add more water as needed). Help them add a few drops of food coloring to the mixture and stir. Make two or three batches, each a different color.

As children help make the finger paint, focus on the changes that are taking place. Talk about the way the mixture looks:

"Andy, watch what happens when you mix the flour and water together. It looks wet and gooey, almost like glue!" Encourage observations as the food coloring is added.

BEGIN

When the finger paint is ready, place several tablespoons of each color on the paper. Invite children to finger-paint over the entire surface. As they work, talk about how the finger paint feels. Comment on the colors they are mixing together. When the finger-paint mural is completed, let the paper dry. Hang at children's eye level so everyone can enjoy!

Remember

▪ Cleanup is easy when a dishpan filled with soapy bubbles is nearby. Set out paper towels and a wastebasket next to the pan.

▪ Add sand to part of the finger paint to make a new texture to feel when painting and to look at when the paint is dry.

▪ For an interesting variation, hang the mural paper on a wall at twos' height. Let them stand in front of the paper, dip hands in the homemade finger paint, and then move up and down and side to side with their whole bodies. Talk about the patterns that evolve from this "movement mural."

BOOKS

Here are books with good art ideas for twos.

▪ *Infant/Toddler: Introducing Your Child to the Joy of Learning* by Earladeen Badger (McGraw-Hill)

▪ *Learning Games for the First Three Years* by J. Sparling and I. Lewis (Berkley Publishing)

▪ *Things to Do With Toddlers and Twos* by Karen Miller (Telshare)

ART

Go brush-crazy with these new painting experiences.

ALL KINDS OF BRUSHES!

Aim: Children will develop new tactile experiences, use small- and large-motor skills, and become aware of and use different body parts.

Group size: One to three children.

Materials: Brown butcher-block paper, tape, tempera paint, plastic foam meat trays, smocks, and an assortment of the following types of brushes: pastry, vegetable, watercolor, makeup, hair, nail, outdoor-paint, scrub, easel, shoe, and wallpaper.

GETTING READY

Show and name the brushes with children. Talk about where they've seen the brushes before. "Do you see brushes that Mommy (or Daddy or Grandma) uses to do work in the house? Do you see brushes we use in school?"

Encourage children to feel the brushes. Ask, "What does it feel like when you touch the brushes?" Try to elicit words such as *hard, soft, scratchy, smooth, rough*, etc. Invite children to show you brushes they would use to brush their hands, and be sure to steer them toward ones with soft bristles. Ask, "Can we brush other parts of our bodies?" Brush arms, elbows, legs, knees, etc.

Tape the butcher-block paper to a table for painting indoors, or on the sidewalk for outdoor painting. Put paint in plastic foam meat trays, and help children put on smocks.

BEGIN

Show children how to put a brush in paint, and then brush-paint the butcher-block paper. Make sure a variety of brushes are available for them to experiment with (though they may only concentrate on one or two types). Encourage children to talk about the designs their brushes make: "Look Sara, the scrub brush makes a larger design than the nail brush."

If the group is painting outdoors, you might also let children use the bigger brushes — large paintbrush, shoe brush, scrub brush, easel paintbrush, wallpaper brush — and a bucket of water to paint the school building and playground with water. This is not only fun for twos; it also helps to foster large-muscle development.

Remember

▪ Twos may want to put a hairbrush in their hair or a toothbrush in their mouths, even when the brushes are full of paint. Supervise carefully and remind them that these brushes are for painting.

▪ Brushes will feel different with paint on them. Touching the brushes to discover that difference is part of the experience.

▪ Twos like to feel independent whenever possible. Keep wet paper towels handy so they can wash their own hands.

▪ Washing the brushes is also a delightful experience for twos. Have buckets or pans with soapy water ready for them to use.

BOOKS

Share these books about body parts.

▪ *Babies' Bodies* by Sally Kilroy (Four Winds Press)

▪ *Aleksandra, Where Is Your Nose?* by Christine Salac Dubow (St. Martin's Press)

▪ *Aleksandra, Where Are Your Toes?* by Christine Salac Dubow (St. Martin's Press)

ART

Twos love to scribble. Here's a great alternative to using crayons!

CHALK SCRIBBLES

Aim: Children will develop self-expression and use fine-motor skills as they experiment with chalk in a variety of ways.

Group size: Three or four children.

Materials: Large pieces of nontoxic dustless chalk in bright colors, small bowls (one per child), newspaper, water, containers, construction paper, sponge, sandpaper, tape, and scrap paper of various sizes and shapes.

In Advance: Cover the worktable with newspaper. Place scraps of paper and chalk on or near the table. Keep pieces of construction paper, a sponge, and containers close by.

GETTING READY

Introduce the chalk at the table. Explain that it is different from crayons but as much fun to draw with! Show children the scraps of paper, and give each child a bowl of chalk. Let them color on the scraps any way they wish. As they are coloring, talk about the colors of chalk they are using and their actions: "Meg, you are using a large piece of yellow chalk. I see the lines you are making on your round piece of paper."

BEGIN

When children have finished scribbling on the scraps, use a wet sponge to dampen a piece of construction paper for each child. (Black paper creates a nice contrast with the colored chalk.) Invite children to try coloring on the damp paper. Describe their actions as they use the chalk. Remind them that they may have to press extra-hard to see their lines. When children have completed their pictures, write their names on the back of the papers, and let dry. As twos work on other drawings, compare the way the chalk looks on wet paper with the way it look on dry paper.

SCRIBBLING ON SANDPAPER

Here's another simple scribbling activity using chalk. Provide large pieces of sandpaper (of different textures, but not too rough). Let children feel the sandpaper. Then tape plain paper over the sandpaper. Give children pieces of chalk, and let them scribble to enjoy the grainy effect.

SCRIBBLING OUTDOORS

Take children outside. Show them how they can make colored scribbles directly on the sidewalk or paved areas. Observe with them how daily use or the next rainfall cleans the sidewalk.

Remember
- Chalk can be as messy as paint. Be sure children wear smocks to protect their clothing.
- Large sidewalk chalk, which can be purchased from school-supply companies, produces brighter colors than chalkboard chalk.
- Let twos experiment with chalk to see what kinds of surfaces it can write on. For example, set out sheets of waxed paper for testing. Be ready for some twos to test hands and arms, too!

BOOKS

| Share these stories of art adventures with twos. | *Chalk Box Story* by Don Freeman (J.B. Lippincott) | *Harold and the Purple Crayon* by Crockett Johnson (Harper & Row) | *Is It Red? Is It Yellow? Is It Blue?* by Tana Hoban (Greenwillow Books) |

ART

Small children love to make tunnels and trails. Enjoy this activity together!

MAKING CUP TRAILS

Aim: Children will use fine- and gross-motor skills as they work with finger paint and paper cups.
Group size: Three or four children.
Materials: Finger paint or nonmenthol shaving cream, food coloring (optional), a smooth tabletop, paper cups, small cars and/or plastic animals and people, and damp sponges (for cleanup).

GETTING READY

Help children into their smocks, roll up their sleeves, and gather around a table. Give each child a small dollop of finger paint or shaving cream, and allow ample time for exploring with the material. Encourage children to cover the entire surface of the table. While they work, talk about how the paint or shaving cream feels and smells: "Mmmm, my fingers feel all slippery. Karla, how do yours feel? What can you smell?" Point out interesting patterns.

BEGIN

Now take a cup and give one to each child. Push yours gently along the tabletop, inviting children to do the same. Ask, "What happens when you push your cup along the table?" (The finger paint piles up on the side of the cup.) "What do you think we should do with all the extra paint?"

Point out the trails that form, and encourage children to experiment by making designs and roads. Give them small cars or plastic animals and people to go along their "roads." (This exercise will reinforce twos' awareness of shape and direction.)

You might want to have extra cups and shaving cream available for more experimenting. Before they tire, help twos rinse the plastic props in a bowl of water, use the cups to scrape the paint and shaving cream off the table, and work together to clean up the remaining bits of paint and cream. (Be sure children rinse hands and arms before going on to other activities.)

Remember

▪ Twos can make trails with fingers, cups, even car wheels. Talk about other objects they might use to make trails.
▪ Talk about the shapes the cup can make. For example, demonstrate how to pat the cup on the painted paper to make circles.
▪ Be prepared to remind twos more than once to wash their hands before going on to the next activity. They need repetition.

BOOKS

Use these books for great art activities.

▪ *Active Learning for Twos* by Harms, Cryer, and Bourland (Addison-Wesley)

▪ *Look at Me* by Carolyn Buhai Haas (CBH Publishing)

▪ *Teaching Terrific Twos and Other Toddlers* by Terry Lynne Graham and Linda Camp (Humanics Learning)

ART

Bring dramatic play outside for some house-painting fun!

PAINTING DAY

Aim: Children will pretend about something familiar.
Group size: Whole group.
Materials: Big brushes, paint rollers, pans, buckets, water to paint with, painters' hats, pictures of house painters or sign painters, large boxes, tempera paint, smocks, mural paper, and medium paintbrushes.
In Advance: Put painting utensils and water outside near a large open space (such as a cement wall, sidewalk, or fence) to form a "water-painting area." In another area outdoors, set up the mural paper, water, tempera paint, smocks, and large boxes.

GETTING READY

Outside, gather children in a circle and share the pictures of the people painting. Talk about what these people are painting and what they paint with. Then invite children to be painters.

BEGIN

Bring children to the water-painting area. Demonstrate how to use each of the utensils to paint the hard surface(s). Now invite interested children to paint with water. As they work, talk about their actions: "Jara, that's a big roller you are painting with. I like watching you move it up and down. You are just like a house painter!"

MORE OUTDOOR PAINTING

After the water painting, invite children to use real paint to cover the boxes and mural paper you have set up. You might tell them that the boxes are houses that need a good paint job. Once the boxes dry, they can be used as dollhouses inside and outside for dramatic play, or as props for other activities.

SING A PAINTING CHANT

As children paint, say this chant with them, repeating it many times:

Painting up.
Painting down.
Painting, painting all around!

Remember

▪ When working outside, twos can't resist painting trees, bushes, even grass. Be prepared for brushes to get dirty as they experiment.
▪ On rainy days, let twos use the paintbrushes inside — without paint or even water. They'll love to paint arms, legs, even faces with clean, dry brushes — and they can do it without creating a mess. Keep clean brushes in a container where children can find and return them on their own.
▪ When twos pretend to paint, encourage language development by asking them to describe the colors they're using. You may find out that a young artist is painting his or her blue pants red and pink!

BOOKS

Share these books about painting and colors with twos.

▪ *Colors* by Leo Lionni (Pantheon)

▪ *If You Take a Paintbrush* by Fulvio Testa (Dial Books)

▪ *Yellow and Pink* by William Steig (Farrar, Straus & Giroux)

ART

Crayons are fun to use, but they're also powerful tools for developing language!

CRAYONS ARE FOREVER

Aim: Through crayon activities, twos will be helped to understand that words can be used to describe tools, materials, and feelings.

Group size: Two or three children.

Materials: Red, yellow, and blue crayons; different kinds of paper (manila, construction, wrapping, newsprint, etc.); and newspaper to protect table from crayon markings.

In Advance: Cover a table with newspaper. Place paper for two or three children on the table. Arrange crayons in containers in the middle of the table.

GETTING READY

Use a book such as one listed below to introduce color words. Let children "read" the pictures. Assist by pointing to different illustrations and asking, "What is this? What color is it?" Then ask, "Can you find a (blue, red, yellow, etc.) crayon?" Ask children to find crayons that match the colors of the objects in the illustrations.

BEGIN

Now encourage children to freely use paper and crayons. Name the materials children choose. For instance: "Jane chose the blue crayon. She chose the manila paper."

Look for "talkable moments" — times when you can talk about what a child is doing without disturbing his or her work. "Mark is pushing his crayon up and down the paper. Casey is moving the crayons round and round on the paper." In turn, encourage the child to use words to describe what he is doing and how the experience makes him feel.

Twos feel secure with the familiar — such as crayons and paper. Keep them coming back for more by adding something new each day. For example, introduce a new place to scribble — on the floor, table, easel, or outside on the sidewalk. Introduce a new position such as standing, sitting, or lying.

SING A SONG OF COLORS

Sing this song with the group about something each child is wearing. It's sung to the tune of "Mary Had a Little Lamb."

Colorful Clothes
Susan wore a yellow shirt, yellow shirt, yellow shirt.
Susan wore a yellow shirt to nursery school today.

Form a circle. Ask each child to come to the center of the circle when the group sings about what he is wearing.

Remember
- Some twos will be confused by too many colors. Stick with primary colors — red, blue, and yellow — since these are the colors most children learn first.
- Planning a day when one particular color is highlighted is a good way to focus twos' attention on colors. After you have planned a few color days, let twos decide what color to highlight next.

BOOKS

Here are some good books about colors to share with children.

- *Is It Red? Is It Yellow? Is It Blue?* by Tana Hoban (Greenwillow Books)
- *My First Book of Things* by John E. Johnson (Random House)
- *Red, Blue, Yellow Shoe* by Tana Hoban (Greenwillow Books)

 ART

Threes can celebrate colors while making some exciting discoveries!

PLAN A PURPLE DAY

Aim: Children will observe, compare, and create colors through a variety of media.
Group size: Three or four children.
Materials: Blue and red homemade playdough (use the recipe in "Creature Features," page 67, or your own); easel paint and paper; and red and blue food coloring.
In Advance: Prepare the homemade playdough.

GETTING READY

Show examples of purple items gathered from around the room. Ask children to name foods that are purple, such as grapes, eggplant, grape jelly, etc. Ask, "Who is wearing something that is purple?" Challenge children to find examples of purple in the room.

BEGIN

An excellent way for threes to experience color mixing is by "smushing" two colors of playdough together. They'll see the color change gradually.

Give each child a small ball of red and a small ball of blue playdough. Don't tell children what will happen when they mix the colors together. Instead, just allow ample time for them to knead, pound, and smash the balls together. Eventually you will hear shouts of, "It's purple!"

Most threes are content to play with the dough without making something. However, you may want to challenge their imaginations to create purple pets, purple people, or other purple creatures.

Another time, try mixing colors for a green day or an orange day.

MORE PURPLE IDEAS
▪ Put shades of purple paint, from dark purple to lavender, at the easel. If possible, supply lavender paper, too.
▪ Surprise children by adding red and blue food coloring to the water in the water table. Squirt some liquid detergent for terrific purple suds!
▪ Serve a purple-colored food for snack.

Remember
▪ As children work, the colors will first be mostly a mixture of red and blue globs. Eventually the spots will merge together and purple swirls will appear. The longer the dough is worked, the more purple it becomes — and the more fine-motor exercise

children get. Eventually it will be all purple, with no red or blue showing. Ask, "Where did the red and blue dough go?"
▪ Mixing colors with threes needs to be an "ah-ha" experience. Give children plenty of opportunities to mix whatever colors they choose, even if they end up with a muddy brown. Through experimentation, threes will discover that too many colors make a mess, helping them become more knowledgeable in their mixing.
▪ Playdough is also a great material for cutting practice. It's sturdier than paper, so beginning cutters are more successful. Be sure to provide right- and left-handed safety scissors.

BOOKS

| Here are some good books about colors. | ▪ *Harold and the Purple Crayon* by Crockett Johnson (Harper & Row) | ▪ *Colors* by Jean Pientowski (Simon & Schuster) | ▪ *The Rainbow* by Mike Thaler (Harlin Quist) |

ART

Turn your playground into an art "exploratorium" with these great activities.

COME TO OUR SIDEWALK ART SHOW!

Aim: Children will participate in two multimedia art activities outdoors.

Group size: Four to six children for each activity.

GETTING READY

Introduce the idea of an art show. Ask, "Have you ever been to an art show? What did you find there?" Expand on children's understanding of an art show as needed. Then talk about children's favorite art activities. Have they done any of these activities outside? Invite them to do some art activities outdoors, then to display their work at a "Sidewalk Art Show." Be sure to invite families to visit the show!

SIDEWALK CHALK ART

Materials: Thick pieces of colored dustless chalk, plastic spray bottles, water, newspaper, and smocks.

BEGIN

Gather the group around a sidewalk that is a safe distance from any street or traffic area. Show children the box of chalk. Ask, "How can we draw with chalk without using paper? What can we draw on?"

Mark off large squares on the sidewalk or blacktop for children to use as their "paper." Give them chalk and encourage them to draw and to experience the different textures of the sidewalk. Some children will enjoy tracing large objects or even each other on the sidewalk.

Provide spray bottles filled with water to add a new dimension to the project. Ask, "What happens when you spray your picture

with just a little water? Do the colors change?" Children can place a sheet of newspaper over their wet drawings, press lightly, and make a print of the pictures. Hang these on a clothesline for the sidewalk art show.

BOX PAINTING

Materials: Large cardboard boxes, egg cartons, inexpensive tempera paint, large house-painting brushes and rollers, coffee cans, smocks, newspaper, a stapler, and other fasteners.

BEGIN

Start this delightful exploration of color and shape by covering an area of the playground with newspaper. Give children large cardboard boxes, paintbrushes, and coffee cans with paint, and let them go!

Children may enjoy stacking their boxes to form "sculptures." Take charge of using the stapler or other fasteners to secure the boxes together once children have decided on the shapes. Display in a "sculpture garden" at your art show.

Remember

▪ Working outside is perfect for threes. They need plenty of space for moving about, for creating, and for getting "messy." Have children wear smocks, and keep a pan of soapy water and paper towels nearby.

▪ In warm weather, do as much as possible outdoors. Water play is a natural, but storytime can go out, too. Bring out large blocks and dramatic-play props, and observe how play takes on a new dimension.

BOOKS

| Share these books that focus on outdoor activities. | ▪ *A Tree Is Nice* by Janice Udry (Harper & Row) | ▪ *At the Park* by Colin McNaughton (Philomel Books) | ▪ *Look in the Yard* by Art Seiden (Grosset & Dunlap) |

ART

Add some spark to the easel with these unusual painting ideas.

EASEL EXCITEMENT

Aim: Children will use expressive and descriptive language as they experiment with different materials.
Group size: Two or three children.
Materials: Easels, easel paper, and other materials as listed under each activity.

GETTING READY

This is a good activity to try when you observe that children are losing interest in painting at the easel. At circle time, talk about painting. Ask children to brainstorm ideas to add to a chart titled "We Can Paint With ... " Encourage them to suggest different items to use in place of paintbrushes and paper. Try some of their suggestions over the next few weeks. You might add the ideas below to the children's as well.

BEGIN

MYSTERY PAINT

Before children arrive, add textured items to paint that has been mixed with a little water and white glue. Include sand, sawdust, glitter, salt, etc. As children paint, ask them if they think the paint is different today. Encourage them to suggest what the "mystery" is. As they work, texture lines from the added ingredients will appear on their papers.

PAINTBRUSH SURPRISES

Provide unusual items to paint with. Here are two ideas to try.
Sponge Painting – Cut a sponge into different-sized pieces. Clip a clothespin "handle" onto each piece. Dish sponges with handles also work well. They make a wonderful snowflake-like print when dipped in white paint and printed on a dark color.
Berry-Basket Painting – Pour paint into a shallow tray, and set out plastic berry baskets. Children can dip the basket into paint, then press onto easel paper.

PAPER WITH PIZZAZZ

Change the types of paper you use. For example, try the classi-fied section of the newspaper. See if children incorporate some of the print into their paintings. Corrugated cardboard creates interest-ing problems to solve as children paint over the bumps. Aluminum foil is an exciting surface to create on with paint that has been mixed with a little white glue.

Remember

▪ Collect dictation from children as they try these new and different ways to paint. Display the pictures and children's words on a low bulletin board.
▪ Threes are typically more interested in spreading paint around the paper than in painting a picture. They are fascinated by the way the paint drips and by new colors that appear when different colors mix.
▪ Threes also like to layer colors. They may complete one "picture," then cover it with a new color of paint. Have plenty of paper available so that children know they can paint more than one picture. Be ready to let threes paint in their own way.

BOOKS

| Share these books with your young artists. | ▪ *Begin at the Beginning* by Amy Schwartz (Harper & Row) | ▪ *The Painter's Trick* by Piero and Marisa Ventura (Random House) | ▪ *Paper, Paper Everywhere* by Gail Gibbons (Harcourt Brace Jovanovich) |

ART

Try this activity to make gifts that will brighten any window.

MAKE "SUN CATCHERS"

Aim: Children will use creative expression and fine-motor skills as they make special gifts.

Group size: Three or four children.

Materials: White glue, colored tissue paper, paper doilies, glitter, plastic margarine-tub lids, yarn or ribbon, lunch-sized paper bags, assorted art materials, and a few commercially made window ornaments.

In Advance: Ask a few children to help you tear the tissue paper or doilies into small pieces. This is a great fine-motor exercise, and threes love to rip!

GETTING READY

Talk with children about giving and receiving gifts. Discuss occasions, such as birthdays or holidays, when they may receive gifts. Ask, "How do you feel when you get a gift? How do you feel when you give a gift?"

Now invite children to make "sun catchers" to give as gifts to family members or to other special people. Display examples of window ornaments, and hold them up to the light so that children can see how they change in color. Talk about the name. Ask, "Why do you think these are called sun catchers? Do you have any in your windows at home? Are there any in our room?"

BEGIN

Set out one lid for each child, as well as the tissue paper, doily scraps, and glitter. Have each child cover the entire lid with white glue. Then let each cover the lid with pieces of tissue and doily and with sprinkles of glitter. If necessary, add more glue so the pieces

stay secure. Be sure to let children select and arrange the pieces any way they want.

Just before the glue is dry, gently pull the lid away from each paper ornament. With a hole puncher, add a hole in the top. Thread a short length of yarn through the hole for hanging. When the glue dries completely, light will shine through the ornament.

MAKE GIFT BAGS

Use lunch-sized paper bags to make gift bags for holding the finished sun catchers. Give each child a paper bag. Set out crayons, glue, collage items, stickers, printmaking materials, and other materials children can use to decorate the bags as they wish. Insert the sun catchers, and gather the bags at the top with ribbon or yarn.

Remember

• Threes' attention spans will vary. Some will want to cover every open space on the lid. Others will be finished when they've pasted on three scraps of tissue. Don't push children to continue with the activity if they've lost interest. Rather, start with different sizes of lids. Give threes with shorter attention spans the smaller lids so they will have less space to cover and still feel successful.

• Even though this is a gift, don't overemphasize the importance of the final product. Let children create in their own way. Resist the temptation to suggest ways to make the sun catchers look "prettier."

• Sun catchers also make great necklaces. Tie on a longer length of yarn to fit easily over the head.

BOOKS

| Share these books about gift-giving with threes. | • *Bobo's Dream* by Martha Alexander (Scholastic) | • *Claude the Dog* by Dick Gackenbach (Clarion) | • *Clifford's Birthday Party* by Norman Bridwell (Scholastic) |

ART

Here's a wonderful fall art experience that threes will find "sense-sational"!

TRIPLE-FUN LEAF PRINTS

Aim: Children will experiment with a variety of sensory experiences while making leaf prints.
Group size: Four to six children.
In Advance: Take a walk together outside to gather fall leaves for making prints. You might also ask children to bring in leaves that they find at home.

GETTING READY

Gather children together to talk about the leaves they collected on the walk or brought from home. Pass around a few leaves for children to touch. Together, compare the sizes, shapes, and textures of the different leaves. Ask interested children to sort the leaves into piles of "big" and "little" leaves. Invite children to use the leaves to make prints.

BEGIN
FINGER-PAINTED LEAF PRINTS
Materials: Leaves, finger paint, newspaper, and white or colored paper.

Show children how to find the bumpy side of the leaf with the raised veins. Demonstrate how to use fingers to spread paint on the leaf. Then have children place the leaf on plain paper, paint side down. Place newspaper over the leaf, and press to make a print. Encourage children to try leaves of different shapes to see the different prints. For a group mural, try this technique on shelf paper or on an old sheet.

ALUMINUM-FOIL PRINTED LEAVES
Materials: Leaves, heavyweight aluminum foil, paste, and construction paper.

Show children how to place a piece of aluminum foil over a bumpy leaf, then gently press and rub to get a print. The process is so intriguing many children will want to do it over and over! Encourage them to try leaves of different shapes and sizes.

LEAF PRINTS IN CLAY
Materials: Leaves, self-hardening water-base clay, waxed paper, rolling pins or cylinder blocks, and yarn.

Give each child a small lump of clay. Have each roll out the clay to a size a little larger than a leaf, and place the bumpy side of the leaf down on the clay. Next, place a sheet of waxed paper over the leaf and clay. Demonstrate how to skim the rolling pin over the waxed paper so that the leaf sinks into the clay. Ask children to carefully remove the paper, pull off the leaf by the stem, and place the clay print in a sunny window to dry. To make a print to hang, make a hole in the clay above the leaf print while it's still moist, and insert a length of yarn when completely dried.

Remember
- Use large leaves with threes to accommodate their limited fine-motor coordination. Choose fresh leaves with sturdy stems. Dried leaves will crack and crumble.
- Enhance language development by encouraging threes to describe how the leaves feel — bumpy, rough, smooth, fuzzy, etc. Reinforce understanding of these words by asking children to locate other objects in the room that are bumpy, smooth, rough, fuzzy, etc.
- For paint and foil activities, tape leaves to the table so that they won't move around as children work.

BOOKS

Share these favorite fall books before or after your leaf-printing activities.	■ *All Falling Down* by Gene Zion (Harper & Row)	■ *Frederick* by Leo Lionni (Pantheon)	■ *The Wonderful Tree* by Adelaide Hall (Golden Press)

ART

Threes will have fun expressing their own creativity with this "monstrous" activity!

MONSTER MIX-UPS

Aim: Children will use creative-thinking, language, and fine-motor skills.

Group size: Three or four children.

Materials: Black construction paper, two or three light colors of tempera paint, plastic squeeze bottles, and markers.

In Advance: Fill squeeze bottles with liquid tempera. (Add a few drops of liquid detergent if the paint is very runny.) Fold a sheet of black paper, reopen, and lay flat. Squirt a moderate amount of paint on the paper, refold, then open to make a paint-blot picture. Repeat to make several pictures to show children.

GETTING READY

Look for *It Looked Like Spilt Milk* by Charles G. Shaw (Harper & Row) to read aloud. Or start with the the paint-blot pictures you have made. Ask, "What does this picture remind you of? Does it look like anything you have seen before?" Some children might see squashed pumpkins, flying bats, or even monsters. Be sure to point out that there is no right answer, and that one child may see something that another doesn't. Then invite children to make their own "mix-up" pictures.

BEGIN

Set out the paper and paints in squeeze bottles. Demonstrate how to slowly squeeze a few lines and dots of paint on one side of the fold. Close on the fold and gently press. Open the paper to view the "mix-up."

Impress upon children the importance of using just a small amount of paint. Reassure them they can make more than one mix-up if they want.

MAKE A MIX-UP PICTURE BOOK

Help threes develop creative-language skills with this activity. When children have completed their pictures, talk about what the children think they are. Challenge them to view the pictures from different angles to check if they see something different.

Point out that pictures often have a "title" or a name that describes what the picture looks like. Invite children to name their pictures. (Avoid the question, "What is it?" Instead, ask, "Do you have a name for your picture?") Take whatever children tell you, whether it's a sentence or one word. Do not press children to name their pictures at all if they don't want to. Then insert the pictures in a photo album with plastic-coated pages. Place the album where children can look at the pictures on their own.

What does it look like?	
monster	David
snowstorm	Meg
butterfly	Pablo

Remember

• Threes love this activity because it's quick, easy, and fun. Be sure to have plenty of paper so that children can continue to make pictures as long as their interest holds.

• Some children may want to take their pictures home instead of having them go into the group book. Don't insist that children contribute to the book.

BOOKS

These books with terrific amorphic shapes will spark more discussions about "mix-ups."

• *The Little Red Ant* by Yvonne Hooker (Grosset & Dunlap)

• *Splodges* by Malcom Carrick (Viking)

• *The Turn About, Think About, Look About Book* by Beau Gardner (Greenwillow Books)

ART

Head for the easel! It's time for a new twist on mixing colors.

MAGIC COLOR SPLOTCHES

Aim: Children will experiment with mixing colors as well as use fine-motor and creative-thinking skills.

Group size: Two children.

Materials: An easel, small plastic spray bottles, colored tissue paper or streamers, heavy white drawing paper, paper plates, and pieces of string (optional).

In Advance: Ask a few children to help you tear the tissue paper or streamers into small pieces. This is a great fine-motor exercise, and this age loves to rip!

GETTING READY

A good time to introduce this activity is when you observe that children are losing interest in easel painting. Explain that they'll be making pictures without using brushes or paint. Show children the paper scraps and the spray bottles, then ask, "How do you think we can use these things to make a picture?"

BEGIN

Set up a small table next to the easels to hold the tissue paper and water bottles. Gather children to watch as you attach a sheet of white paper to an easel and spray water on it. Next, invite children to stick the colored scraps onto the paper. Ask, "What do you think will happen when we put the colored water on the wet paper?" Encourage children to mix different-colored scraps together by placing two or three different colors on top of one another. Demonstrate how to use fingers to flatten the scraps onto the white paper.

Spray water lightly over the picture again. Then ask children to take off the colored scraps. A colorful picture will appear! Look together for places where the colors have mixed and talk about the new colors.

MAKE CLASSROOM DECORATIONS

To make decorations, use the same technique. Ask children to place the colored tissue scraps on a paper plate, and then spray the plate. Remove the scraps, make a hole at the top of the plate, insert yarn for hanging, and you have a room decoration. Try experimenting with two primary colors at a time. Encourage children to guess the new color that will appear.

Remember

▪ Write children's names on the back of their papers. When adults write on children's artwork, they interfere with the child's view of the work. Threes don't see their name as part of the picture. When displaying finished artwork, write children's names on file cards and attach to the bulletin board near their pictures.

▪ Try to use tissue paper instead of crepe paper for this activity. The colors are more pastel.

▪ If you have extra torn paper left over, keep it for other projects. For example, on another day, glue it to paper plates that have been "painted" with white glue. The paper will stick easily and overlap to form new colors. Invite children to paste the paper flat or wadded up into little balls. Threes love to wad!

BOOKS

Share these books about colors with children.	▪ *I Want to Paint My Bathroom Blue* by Ruth Krauss (Harper & Row)	▪ *Little Blue and Little Yellow* by Leo Lionni (Astor-Honor)	▪ *Mouse Paint* by Ellen Stoll Walsh (Harcourt Brace Jovanovich)

ART

Threes will enjoy finger-painting with new or old friends.

SHARE COLORS WITH A FRIEND

Aim: Children will experiment with mixing colors while interacting with a partner.

Group size: Three or four children.

Materials: A plastic tablecloth or a long sheet of freezer or shelving paper, and two to four colors of finger paint.

In Advance: Be sure to have a smooth surface ready for children to paint on, such as a formica tabletop. Cover the table with the freezer or shelving paper, taping securely in place.

GETTING READY

Explain that today threes are going to finger-paint in a special way — as a group. Instead of each child having his or her own piece of paper, groups will work together on one big table or giant piece of paper. The result will be a cooperative masterpiece.

BEGIN

Help each child find a place to stand around the table. Give

everyone a glob of paint, each a different color, if possible. Encourage children to try new ways to paint by asking, "What other ways can we paint with our hands?" They may try using their fists, one finger, or the sides of their hands.

Suggest that they spread their paint to mix with the paint of the person next to them or across the table. Ask, "What happens when your two colors meet? Did the colors change? How many different colors do we have now?" Try to record the children's comments as they make discoveries about color mixing.

Hang finished murals on a wall. Nearby, post the children's comments, written on chart paper.

MAKE "MAGIC MIXING BAGS"

Materials: Zip-lock plastic storage bags (freezer bags are the strongest), powdered tempera paint, liquid laundry starch, and masking tape.

In Advance: Partially prepare the bags by measuring 1/4 cup of starch and three tablespoons each of two different colors of powdered tempera into each plastic bag. Close the bag with the zip-lock seal, making sure excess air is squeezed out. Cover the seal with masking tape to prevent leaks.

BEGIN

Give each child a bag, and let the fun begin! Encourage children to squeeze their bags gently to mix the paint and starch. As they squeeze, talk about the different colors that form. For more experimentation, have each child place the bag on the table, then use fingers to trace lines and shapes in the paint.

Remember

▪ Threes are just beginning to cooperate. Typically, children will do art projects next to each other without much interaction. This activity is a great way to encourage children to work together, but you may have to model cooperation by mixing colors with one child. Be careful not to push the interaction.

▪ Some threes don't like to get "messy" and shy away from activities like finger-painting. The magic mixing bags are a "clean" way to involve children in color mixing. After this activity, have them paint with colored water on paper before they try finger paint.

BOOKS

Celebrate color with these stories.

▪ *The Magic of Color* by Heidi Simin (Lothrop, Lee & Shepard)

▪ *The Mystery of the Stolen Blue Paint* by Steven Kellogg (Dial Books)

▪ *The Night the Crayons Talked* by Vicki Knight (Borden)

 ART

Ready, set, spray! Here's a great cooperative art activity for threes.

LET'S MAKE A SPRAY-ART MURAL

Aim: Children will use fine-motor, creative-thinking, problem-solving, and social-interaction skills.
Group size: Three or four children.
Materials: Spray bottles filled with thinned tempera paint in compatible colors, and mural paper or large sheets of newsprint.

GETTING READY

Show the spray bottles to children. Talk about how to use them and especially the importance of spraying paint only on the paper. Take time to demonstrate the correct method and the various effects of short bursts and long, sweeping sprays.

BEGIN

Attach a large sheet of mural paper to a low wall. Then place newspapers on the floor beneath it. Invite two children to stand a few feet apart and spray the paint on the paper. With both in agreement, encourage them to slowly approach each other's paintings and overlap their colors. Talk about the changes in the picture by asking, "What happens when Marta's paint mixes with Joseph's? What would happen if you traded places?" Involve one or two more children and suggest that they try different hand and arm motions. Encourage everyone to talk about their creation.

MAKE A LEAF MURAL

Go outside together and collect a variety of fresh leaves and grasses. Back inside, place a sheet of mural paper on the floor on top of newspaper. Invite children to place their leaves and grasses on the paper in various designs and patterns. (You may need to lightly tape down the leaves.) Now ask children to stand above the mural paper and try spray-painting around the leaves. When the paint is dry, help children remove the leaves and enjoy the discovery of interesting silhouettes.

Remember

- Hang the murals where family members can enjoy and comment on them. During circle time, invite everyone to talk about the work. Encourage group pride in this joint creative effort. Next time, invite family members to help.
- Spraying a friend is tempting, so frequently review with threes the safe way to use the spray bottles. Demonstrate how to hold the bottle and aim the nozzle at the paper.
- On a warm day, take the spray bottles outside to make water paintings on sidewalks, walls — almost any dry surface.
- Introduce the spray bottle at the sand table. Threes are fascinated by the patterns the water can make in sand.

BOOKS

Share these books about colors and painting with threes.	▪ *Colors* by Leo Lionni (Pantheon)	▪ *Mouse Paint* by Ellen Stohl Walsh (Harcourt Brace Jovanovich)	▪ *Little Blue and Little Yellow* by Leo Lionni (Astor)

ART

Threes will have fun creating their own cloud formations on paper.

CLOUDY-DAY PICTURES

Aim: Children will experiment with moving air as they create cloud pictures.

Group size: Three or four children.

Materials: Dark blue and purple construction paper, white tempera paint (thinned with water), eyedroppers, and straws.

GETTING READY

On a warm cloudy day, take children outside to observe the clouds. As they lie on their backs on the ground, encourage them to look for images in the clouds. Ask, "What do you see in the clouds? Animals? Faces?" Point out how the clouds move across the sky, and explain that air makes them move. Later, discuss the experience and record comments on chart paper.

BEGIN

Tell children that they are going to make their own clouds on paper. Introduce the art materials. Explain that they'll use white paint to make the clouds. The straws and their breath will act like the air that makes the clouds "move" across the paper. Show children how to use the eyedroppers to place paint on a corner of the paper. Demonstrate how to blow through the straw to move the drop of paint across the paper.

Then ask children to add another "cloud drop" of paint and to pretend to be the wind again. Encourage them to blow from a different direction. Continue until each child has a few clouds on the paper.

Now have children talk about their clouds. Ask, "Do you see anything in your clouds like we saw in the ones outside? What do your clouds look like?" Record their ideas on a separate piece of paper. Display with the pictures on a wall.

LET THE WIND BE THE ARTIST

Here's a great activity for an especially windy day. Go outside and help children note how hard the wind is blowing by the way it blows their hair, clothing, etc. Explain that each child will help the wind be an artist. Provide each with white paper and a few drops of colored tempera (it should be fairly thick but not runny). Check to see which way the wind is blowing. Then have children hold their papers to catch the wind and let the breeze create a design. Talk about the designs the wind has made. Display on a "Look What the Wind Did!" bulletin board in the room.

Remember

▪ Threes may need help using the eyedroppers. Observe children carefully and demonstrate how to fill them with paint as assistance is needed.

▪ The key to doing great straw-blowing pictures is the angle at which the straw is held over the paint. If a child holds the straw upright, directly over the paint, it will only splatter a little. But if a child kneels down and blows across the paper, the paint will move in many directions to create wonderful designs. This is a fun activity to share with parents and other family members.

▪ After observing clouds outside, put on some airy music inside. Invite threes to move like puffy clouds. Add white streamers or scarves to the experience, too.

BOOKS

Share these books about clouds and wind.

▪ *Hello Clouds!* by Dalia Renberg (Harper & Row)

▪ *Please, Wind?* by Carol Greene (Children's Press)

▪ *Sky Dog* by Brinton Turkle (Follette)

ART

Paint with ice? Fours will be amazed!

ICICLE PAINTING

Aim: Children will practice observation and prediction skills as they experiment with a new painting technique.

Group size: Four or five children.

Materials: Ice-cube tray, popsicle sticks, food coloring or shavings of different colors of dustless chalk, newspaper, and finger-paint or freezer-wrap paper.

In Advance: Prepare the ice-cube "paintbrushes" the night before the activity. Fill the ice-cube tray with water. Insert a popsicle stick in each cube. (Don't worry if the sticks don't stand up straight.)

GETTING READY

Invite fours to share what they know about ice. Ask, "What does ice look like? What does it feel like if you touch it?" Discuss what ice is — frozen water — and what happens to ice when it gets warm.

BEGIN

Cover the work area with newspaper. Give each child a piece of paper and an ice cube "paintbrush." Encourage children to rub the ice cubes across the shiny paper. Then have them sprinkle on different-colored shavings of chalk. Watch for children's reactions as the ice melts and the colors mix.

As a variation, add food coloring in different shades to the ice-cube water before freezing. In the wintertime in cold climates, children can even try painting with real icicles, but be sure they work with gloves on!

Remember

▪ Fours are beginning to understand the concept of melting. Most know that as ice gets warm, it turns to water. Ask children to make predictions about which ice cube would melt the fastest: one in the refrigerator, one on the windowsill, or one on the radiator. Test their predictions.

▪ Play "icicle freeze tag." While music plays, children move like flowing water. But when the music stops, they freeze into an ice shape. When it starts again, they melt into water again.

▪ If you live in a snowy climate and have access to fresh, clean snow, turn your water table into a snowbox. Fill it with snow, positioning it away from sunny windows or other warm areas of the room. Then have children wear smocks and gloves as they "play" in the snow indoors!

BOOKS

Share these wintry stories with fours.

▪ *Bear Weather* by Lillie Chaffin (Macmillan)

▪ *Buzzy Bear's Winter Party* by Dorothy Marino (Franklin Watts)

▪ *Slush, Slush* by Ethel and Leonard Kessler (Parents Magazine Press)

 ART

These printing projects give fours some "hands-on" experience with opposites.

OPPOSITE PRINTING

Aim: Children will observe and identify opposites as they make prints.

Group size: Three or four children.

Materials: Construction paper, tempera paint (mixed with a little liquid detergent), brushes or rollers, plastic foam trays, popsicle sticks, white glue, and rectangles of heavy cardboard.

GETTING READY

Talk about simple opposites and invite children to demonstrate a few. For example, can they point up, then down? Make a loud noise, then a soft noise? Use props to demonstrate other opposites such as big and little.

BEGIN

Give each child a plastic foam tray. Help each find the top and

bottom of the tray. Next, have children flip the trays so that the bottom side is facing up. Ask them to use the popsicle sticks to "etch" or press designs into the backs of the soft foam trays. Ask them to roll or brush paint over their designs.

Now press paper on top of each tray to make a print. Remove the paper to see a print with a design that is an "opposite" of the design on the tray. A dark-colored paper and a light-colored paint work best and give you the chance to talk about light and dark as opposites.

MORE OPPOSITE PRINTS

Try glue printing for another "opposite" effect. A day ahead of time, have children use white glue to create patterns on heavy cardboard. They should apply the glue quite thickly so that the designs have dimension. Let the glue dry overnight.

To make the prints, each child brushes or rolls paint over the glue design, covers it with a sheet of paper, presses firmly, then carefully lifts off the paper. Encourage children to compare the design on the print with the original glue design.

SAY AN OPPOSITE CHANT

Enhance awareness of opposite words with this chant. Invite children to add verses for opposites they know.

> *I can say yes*
> *And I can say no.*
> *I can say fast*
> *And I can say slow.*
>
> *I can say bottom*
> *And I can say top.*
> *I can start*
> *And I can STOP!*

Remember

■ Some fours may need more concrete experiences with opposites. Play a movement game where children stand, then sit; look up, then down; run fast, then slow.

■ The concept of opposites is an exciting one for fours. Encourage them to look for other opposites — in colors, sizes, actions, sounds — as they work and play, and supply the words that describe those opposites.

BOOKS

Add these books to your discussions of opposites.

■ *Antonyms: Hot and Cold and Other Words That Are Different as Day and Night* by Joan Hanson (Lerner)

■ *Big and Little, Up and Down* by Ethel Berkley (Addison-Wesley)

■ *Push-Pull, Empty-Full* by Tana Hoban (Macmillan)

ART

Turn your fours into artists — with a little help from the wind!

WIND-POWERED PAINTING

Aim: Children will use creative-thinking and problem-solving skills as they experiment with air and paint.

Group size: Four to six children.

Materials: Large sheets of newspaper or white paper, thinned tempera paint, tape, pingpong or small plastic foam balls, shallow pans, straws, and mural paper.

GETTING READY

This is a good activity to bring out on a windy day. Talk about the wind and what it feels like blowing against hair, faces, and bodies. Review with children that wind is moving air. Challenge

them to show how they can create moving air, such as by blowing air with their mouths, waving their arms, or spinning their bodies. Talk about machines that make air, such as fans and hair dryers, and, if possible, have some on hand to demonstrate.

BEGIN

Tape the sheets of paper to the worktable so they won't blow away during this "windy" project. Spread extra newspaper on the floor around the worktable to protect it from paint-covered balls that may fall off the table. Pour paint into the shallow pans. Then set out the pans and the balls. Ask, "How can we use these things to paint on our papers without using our hands? Can wind we make with our mouths help?"

Have children dip pingpong balls in paint, then place them on their paper. Challenge fours to use straws to blow the balls so that they leave a trail of paint on the paper. Encourage each to try different colors and to blow the balls in different directions. Ask, "What would happen if you blew two balls at once? Can you draw lines and shapes with the balls?"

MAKE A MURAL

Tape a large sheet of mural paper to the table for making a group wind mural. Have children take turns using straws to blow paint-covered balls across the paper. But to add more challenge and excitement to the activity, ask children to first predict how far their balls will travel. With a pencil, mark the predicted distance for each ball. Then have them blow the balls and check how close they come. Talk about how they might make the balls go farther, such as by blowing harder. After experimenting with predicting lengths, encourage children to fill up the paper with "windy paint trails" in a variety of colors. Display the mural with the title "Wind-Powered Painting."

Remember

▪ Look for other ways to develop children's skills at predicting. For example, together, brainstorm other ways they might create wind, such as by fanning the balls with their hands or with a homemade fan. Invite children to predict which method will work best, then test the methods to check their predictions.

▪ For another kind of predicting activity, gather small objects from around the room, such as a block, crayon, water-play toy, etc. Ask children to predict which objects can be moved by blowing on them through a straw. Test the items to check the predictions.

BOOKS

Share these books about the wind with fours.

▪ *Curious George Flies a Kite* by Margaret Rey (Houghton Mifflin)

▪ *Jonathan Plays With the Wind* by Kathryn Galleant (Coward-McCann)

▪ *The Red Balloon* by Albert Lamorisse (Doubleday)

ART

Sand and art are a natural for fours!

SANDBOX ART

Aim: Children will use fine-motor and creative-thinking skills and self-expression as they use sand as an art medium.
Group size: Four to six children.

GETTING READY

Invite children to share their experiences playing in sand at home, at school, or on a beach. Ask, "Where can you find sand? What can you do with sand? How does sand feel?" Make an experience chart of their ideas.

BEGIN

SAND CASTING
Materials: Outdoor or indoor sandbox; sand; small shovels, scoops, and spoons; small rocks or gravel; water; putty or plaster of paris; mixing containers; popsicle sticks; and a watering can.

This activity can be done inside but it's better as an outdoor activity. Gather children around the sandbox. Have them use the watering can to dampen an area of sand. Then invite them to make designs in the sand with sticks, rocks, and other objects.

Now tell children that today they're going to make permanent pictures in the sand. Use popsicle sticks to fence off an area of the sandbox for each child's sand casting. When children have had time to experiment with designs, ask them to make a design to save.

In a container, mix the water and putty to the consistency of whipped cream. Work fast because the mixture dries quickly. Pour it over each sand design, and let dry overnight. Then remove the casting and have the child brush off the excess sand.

SANDBOX COLLAGES
Materials: White glue in squeeze-top containers, plastic foam trays, plain or colored gravel or pebbles, sand, and yarn.

Have children draw designs with glue on the trays, sprinkle on sand and gravel, then shake off the excess. Let the glue dry completely, punch a hole in the top of each tray, and add yarn for hanging.

MAKE YOUR OWN SAND
Use this activity to show that sand comes from natural objects like rocks and stones. Ahead of time, gather some soft or crumbly stones. Place in a coffee can with a lid. Invite children to take turns shaking the coffee can to break up the stones inside. Check periodically, then when the stones are quite broken down, examine the

sand that has been made. Encourage children to compare this sand with the sandbox sand.

Remember
▪ Be sure each child has plenty of space for creating when doing the sand casting. You may need to set up a second sandbox or do this activity over several days so that each child has a chance to create a casting.
▪ Discourage children from trying to make a cast of a tall, castle-like building. The plaster will slip off and the cast will not be very successful. Flat or indented designs work best because the plaster easily covers or fills in the design.

BOOKS

Share these books about beach days.	▪ *Beach Day* by Helen Oxenbury (Dial Books)	▪ *One Sun* by Bruce McMillan (Holiday House)	▪ *Titus Bear Goes to the Beach* by Renate Kozikowski (Harper & Row)

ART

These open-ended activities will give fours lots of cutting practice.

SNIP, SNIP, CUT, CUT

Aim: Children will develop eye-hand coordination and fine-motor skills as they use scissors to cut a variety of materials.

Group size: Four or five children.

Materials: Safety scissors for right- and left-handed children (or look for the new type that can be used by all children); paste or glue; and items to cut, such as paper straws, wallpaper scraps, stiff paper, plastic foam trays, paper plates, and playdough.

GETTING READY

Place the materials on the table where children will be working. Demonstrate how to open and close the thumb and forefinger to simulate a pair of scissors in motion. Have children try this motion first with their hands, then with a pair of scissors.

BEGIN

Show children the different materials available for cutting. Explain that they can cut any way they wish and that they don't have to make anything.

Guide children toward cutting the sturdier items first, such as the straws, playdough, and plastic foam trays. It's best for novice cutters to work with items that don't flop when placed between the scissors. As children cut, ask, "Can you cut big pieces? Small pieces? Can you make long pieces? Short pieces?" Each should have a paper plate for holding the cut pieces.

When children have exhausted their interest in cutting, give them the option of making a collage from the pieces on their paper plate.

SING A CUTTING SONG

Here's a song to sing as children practice cutting. It's to the tune of "Open, Shut Them." Add scissor-cutting motions as children sing "open, shut."

> *Open, shut them.*
> *Open, shut them.*
> *This is how we cut.*
> *Open, shut them.*
> *Open, shut them.*
> *See how well we cut.*

Remember

▪ Fours love cutting practice, especially when they feel free to cut

without having to follow a line or create a finished product. Open-ended cutting activities help them learn the mechanics of cutting and help small muscles feel the process.

▪ Fours often vary widely in their cutting ability. Make open-ended cutting practice a frequent art choice, especially at the beginning of the year. As children become more adept at cutting, challenge them by introducing line and pattern cutting.

▪ Be sure the scissors children use are safe and easy to handle. Molded plastic scissors are better than metal because they open and close more smoothly and are easier for novice cutters to control. The scissors should be sharp enough to cut paper but designed so that children will not easily cut themselves.

BOOKS

| Here are other art-activity books for small hands. | ▪ *Art and Creative Development* by Robert Schirrmacher (Delmar Publishers) | ▪ *Don't Move the Muffin Tins* by Bev Bos (Turn-the-Page Press) | ▪ *Scribble Cookies* by Mary Ann F. Kohl (Gryphon House) |

ART

Teach fours the ancient art of batik with this simple technique.

CRAYON-AND-PAPER BATIK

Aim: Children will use fine-motor, listening, and sequencing skills, develop self-expression, and practice following directions.
Group size: Three or four children.
Materials: Crayons, heavy white drawing paper (newsprint or other lightweight paper will not work), brown tempera paint, paintbrushes, dishpan of water, and examples of batik cloth (optional).

GETTING READY

Play a quick "follow the directions" game. Have children listen to directions you give and perform them in order. Start with simple two-step directions: Touch your nose; touch your toes. Progress to more difficult patterns: Stand up; shake hands with a friend; spin around; sit down.

Afterward, review the importance of following directions. Talk about activities children do at home or school that involve following directions. Ask, "What happens when you don't follow directions?" Then talk about why some activities are done in a certain order or sequence. Ask, "What would happen if you got into the bathtub before you took off your clothes?" Identify activities at school that are done in a certain sequence, such as cooking snacks.

BEGIN

Introduce the art technique of batik, and, if possible, show some examples of batik cloth. Explain that today children are going to make their own version of batik. Point out that it's important to lis-

ten to your directions because a certain order of steps has to be followed for this project.

Start by having children draw a design with crayon on the heavy white paper. Encourage them to press hard to make thick, dark lines. The process works best if papers are filled with lots of color.

Now place each drawing in a pan of water. Let it sit for a few seconds, then remove. Have children gently crumple the wet paper into a ball. This will give it the crinkled batik look.

Next, have children open the crumpled paper and lightly brush each with brown tempera paint. Then place the paper back in the water to rinse off the paint. When removed, the paper will have a batik-like crackled look.

Let the paper dry completely. Mount on colored construction paper to display.

Remember

▪ Be sure children feel free to make any kind of design on the paper. A representational drawing is not necessary. In fact, large amorphous and geometrical shapes show the batik-like crackle effect best.
▪ Don't let the paper get too wet. If it absorbs too much water it will become squishy and will be difficult to open. If a paper appears too soggy, don't submerge it the second time. Use a paper towel to blot off the brown paint instead of rinsing in the water.

BOOKS

| Here are other books that have unusual art techniques to try with fours. | ▪ *Crayon Crafts and Projects* by Kathy Faggella (First Teacher Press) | ▪ *Don't Move the Muffin Tins* by Bev Bos (Turn-the-Page Press) | ▪ *1-2-3 Art* by Jean Warren (Totline Press) |

ART

Turn fours' imaginations loose with plaster sculptures and see what they create!

PLASTER-SCULPTURE CREATIONS

Aim: Children will use creative thinking and imagination as they form sculptures.

Group size: Three or four children.

Materials: Plaster of paris, water, large paper cups, self-sealing plastic sandwich bags (one per child), masking tape, markers, measuring cups and spoons, plastic spoons, a small lump of clay, and index cards.

GETTING READY

Show children some clay and talk about the kinds of things they can make with clay. Pass around the lump of clay, and ask children to describe how it looks and feels. Then make a simple clay sculpture as children watch. As you work, explain how you are shaping and changing the look of the clay. Then tell children that today they are going to use something similar to clay to make their own creations.

BEGIN

First make the modeling plaster for each child. Measure two tablespoons of water and four tablespoons of plaster of paris into a cup. Mix the ingredients thoroughly. Then pour the mixture into one corner of a plastic bag. Close the bag and let the mixture set for a few minutes. Add masking tape across the self-seal to keep plaster from oozing out. Repeat, making one bag for each participating child.

When the mixture has set but not hardened, invite children to squeeze the outside of the bags to shape the mixture inside. Let them squish the plaster into a person, creature, or just a free-form shape. Open the bags so air can get to the finished shapes, and let them dry completely. Allow at least 30 minutes before removing the objects. Provide markers for children to decorate their sculptures, if desired.

Finally, look at the plaster creations together. Invite children to talk about what they made and about how the plaster felt as they squished and molded it in the bag. Record each child's comments.

A SCULPTURE EXHIBIT

Choose an area of the room to display the plaster creations. Place an index card next to each sculpture that identifies the creator and lists his or her comments about the creation. Invite families to enjoy the display.

Remember

- Plaster of paris dries quickly, so you may want to work with one child at a time while others watch. This will give the watchers a better idea of what to do when it's their turn. Be sure to let children create in their own way once the plaster is in the bags.
- Play a related movement game. Have children pair up. One is the "sculptor," the other the "plaster." As you play soft music in the background, the sculptor slowly arranges the other child's arms, legs, hands, head, etc. into a "sculpture." Then have the pairs change roles.

BOOKS

Share these books about other kinds of changes with your sculptors.

- *It Looked Like Spilt Milk* by Charles Shaw (Harper & Row)
- *Little Blue and Little Yellow* by Leo Lionni (Astor-Honor)
- *Look Again* by Tana Hoban (Macmillan)

ART

Fours will think it's raining colors with this cooperative art project.

IT'S RAINING RAINBOWS!

Aim: Children will experiment with color mixing and the effects of gravity.

Group size: Four to six children.

Materials: Large sheet of white mural or freezer paper, primary-colored tempera paint (thinned with water), large paintbrushes, colored paper streamers, white drawing paper, spray bottles, and glue.

GETTING READY

A rainy day is an ideal time to introduce this activity. Ask, "What happens when you leave something out in the rain? When it gets wet, how does it change? What would happen to a painting if you left it out in the rain?" Record children's ideas on chart paper. If it's raining outside, experiment with a painting that you make or with one that a volunteer offers. Check the results with children's predictions.

BEGIN

Now invite children to make their own "rain" with paint. Ask them to help tape newspaper on an open area of the floor. Tape a large section of white mural paper on top of the newspaper. Place jars of thinned tempera paint around the mural paper. Gather children around the edge of the paper and have them dip their brushes into the paint. As necessary, show them how to let the paint fall onto the paper in drops to create a spattering effect. Discuss what happens when the "paintdrops" hit the paper. Ask, "How do they change?"

Invite children to try different colors. Then ask, "What happens when two different-colored paintdrops splash together?" Challenge children to try different ways of making drops — such as by using brushes of different sizes or by dripping from different heights. Encourage them to fill up the entire paper.

As they work, record children's comments. Display the finished mural, and ask children to describe it.

IT'S A WASHOUT!

At the easel, experiment with washing out colors with water. Place a sheet of paper on the easel. Rip pieces of streamer and lightly glue them to the top of the paper. Then have children spray water on the streamers. As the streamers get wetter and wetter, the colors will run onto the white paper, creating an interesting rain-like effect. Talk about which colors start to run first. Observe if any colors mix as they run. Ask, "What new colors have you made?"

Let children title the picture, if desired. Then display it.

Remember

▪ Fours are much more aware of the effects of mixing colors than threes. Instead of being surprised when colors mix, they expect it. Their curiosity is aroused by the colors that are created. But don't expect fours to know that blue and yellow make green, red and blue make purple, etc. The idea that colors mix and make new colors is the more important understanding now.

▪ Some fours may discover the joys of flicking the paintbrush. This makes a terrific effect but is messy. Try having everyone stand on the same side of the paper and flick away from others.

BOOKS

Share these rainy-day books with fours.	▪ *Plink-Plink* by E. Kessler (Doubleday)	▪ *Rain Rain River* by Uri Shulevitz (Farrar, Straus & Giroux)	▪ *Umbrella* by Taro Yashima (Viking Penguin)

ART

Be ready on the next sunny day to try out this exciting "solar" art!

ART FOR A SUNNY DAY

Aim: Children will use fine-motor skills and creative expression as they experiment with different media.
Group size: Four or five children.

GETTING READY

Gather children for a discussion of activities they like to do on a sunny day. Make an experience chart for recording their responses. Draw a yellow sun in the center, then write children's ideas on the rays. Can they think of art projects to do on a sunny day?

BEGIN

MAKE "SUN CLAY"
Materials: Cooking pot, mixing bowl, large mixing spoon, measuring cup, plastic bag, and plastic trays or paper plates.
Ingredients: 2 cups salt, 1 cup cornstarch, and water.
In Advance: Prepare the sun clay by placing the salt and 2/3 cup water in a saucepan. Cook over medium heat for four to five minutes, stirring until the salt is dissolved. Remove from heat. In a separate bowl, slowly add 1/2 cup water to the cornstarch. Stir until smooth, then add to the salt mixture. Return to low heat and cook until smooth, stirring frequently. Store in a sealed plastic bag. You'll find that when this clay hardens in the sun, it won't crumble like playdough.

Provide children with plastic trays or paper plates to work on outdoors or in a sunny area of the room. Give each child a lump of clay to model. Encourage them to look for natural objects outside, such as small stones, leaves, and dandelions, to use to decorate their sun sculptures. Place the finished items in the sun to dry. Challenge children to predict how long it will take for the sculptures to dry.

BUBBLE PAINTING
Materials: Liquid detergent, water, plastic gallon jugs, shallow pans or pie plates, tempera paint, art paper, and straws.
In Advance: Mix 1/2 cup tempera paint with 1/2 cup detergent in a jug filled with water. Stir and let stand overnight. Make as many colors as you like.

Move a small table outside or set up in a low-traffic area of the playground. Be sure children practice blowing *out* through a straw. Have them place their hands at one end of the straw so that they can feel the air coming out. Then help children pour the paint mixture into the pans, insert their straws, and start blowing bubbles. When a mountain of suds is formed, gently place paper over the bubbles. As they pop, the bubbles will leave wonderful designs.

Remember
▪ Fours' fine-motor coordination is developed enough that they can learn to roll clay into cylinders, even balls. Demonstrate how to take a small amount of clay and roll it between two hands. Children will have difficulty at first but should catch on quickly. But be sure to give them plenty of time to experiment, and don't expect them to model something representational.

BOOKS

Share these stories outdoors on a sunny day.	▪ *Frog and Toad Together* by Arnold Lobel (Scholastic)	▪ *Wake Up, Jeremiah* by Ann Himler (Harper & Row)	▪ *The Wonderful Tree* by Adelaide Hall (Golden Press)

ART

When fours create their own animals, imaginations run wild!

CREATURE FEATURES

Aim: Children will use creative-thinking and language skills as they create animals from art materials.

Group size: Four to six children.

Materials: Playdough (see recipe below), scissors, plastic knives, straws, toothpicks, buttons, egg-carton pieces, small pebbles, wallpaper scraps, small paper plates, and assorted collage materials.

Ingredients: 2 cups self-rising flour, 2 tablespoons alum, 2 tablespoons salt, 2 tablespoons oil, 1 cup plus 2 tablespoons boiling water, and food coloring.

In Advance: Prepare the playdough. Combine the ingredients, except the food coloring, and mix well. Add the food coloring, then knead. To keep soft, place in a sealed container (dough will harden if exposed to the air for a length of time). The dough has an elastic quality that makes it good for modeling. Be sure to use self-rising flour; regular won't work.

GETTING READY

Invite children to talk about animals and pets — those they have at home or would like to have. Ask, "If you could create your own pretend pet, what would it be? What would you call it?" Provide time for children to share their imaginary pets.

BEGIN

Set out the playdough and give children plenty of time to play with it freely. When you observe that children have had adequate time for experimentation, bring out the other art materials. Encourage children to use the dough and materials to create a friendly creature or pet. For example, buttons might become eyes, scales, or belly buttons; toothpicks can be hair, quills, or teeth. As they finish their creatures, place them on a shelf to dry.

CREATURE FEATURES

Enhance language development by asking children to describe the creatures and their special features and to give them names. Ask children to tell how their creature moves, what sounds it makes, where it lives, and what it eats. Write each child's comments on a folded file card to display next to the figure. For example: "This is Snuggalus. He eats plants and lives in a warm hole. He likes to hug things. He likes to sing. By Brandon." Be sure to invite families to "meet" their children's creatures!

Remember

▪ Fours are at a heightened stage of creative thinking. They are excellent pretenders and good at creating fantasies. Capitalize on their vivid imaginations by providing an exciting assortment of accessory materials to add to the playdough. Don't tell children how to use the materials — they'll come up with their own wonderful ideas!

▪ As children sculpt, encourage them to talk about what they are doing and about the creatures they are making. But be careful not to disturb children's concentration as they work. Look for the right moments to engage them in conversation.

BOOKS

| Share these animal books to spark imaginations. | ▪ *Can I Keep Him?* by Steven Kellogg (Dial Press) | ▪ *If I Weren't Me ... Who Would I Be?* by Pam Adams (Child's Play) | ▪ *No Ducks in Our Bathtub* by Martha Alexander (Dial Books) |

ACTIVITY PLAN
READY-TO-USE TEACHING IDEAS FOR FIVES

ART

Bring the colors and wonders of spring indoors!

A SPRING DAY MURAL

Aim: Children will interpret the seasonal changes of spring through creative expression.
Group size: Three or four children.
Materials: Mural paper, markers, crayons, paper cupcake liners, tissue paper, pipecleaners, seed catalogs, cotton balls, construction paper, scissors, and glue.

GETTING READY

Gather the whole group for a discussion about spring. Talk about changes in nature that mark the spring season, such as budding flowers, insects, birds returning from their winter homes, fluffy clouds, and new leaves on trees. Record children's ideas on chart paper. If possible, have some pictures on hand of spring flowers such as daisies, daffodils, and pussy willows.

Now turn children's attention to the idea of creating a spring mural. Review the chart with their responses, and ask children what they would include in a big picture about spring. Show them the materials you've gathered. Talk about which items might make good clouds, which might make good flowers, etc. Be sure to point out that children can use any material in any way they like.

BEGIN

Tape a sheet of mural paper to the floor or to a wall at children's height. Put all art materials on a nearby table. Only a few children at a time should work on the mural. They can make items at the table to glue to the mural or use markers to draw directly on it. Don't worry if a coherent scene is not the result. It's more important for each child to feel free to be expressive in his or her own way.

SPRING STORIES

Follow up the finished mural by inviting children to make up stories about the plants, animals, people, and objects in the scene. Record the stories on chart paper and hang around the mural. Invite families to enjoy your spring display.

Remember

▪ Fives are at a transitional stage in terms of artistic abilities. Some are capable of making representational drawings with great detail, others will make line drawings, and some may still be scribbling. Be sure all styles of drawing are accepted and respected in your room.
▪ To accommodate their varying dexterity, provide children with

different ways to make abstract and representational figures of clouds, flowers, etc. For example, children might make sponge prints or collage flowers instead of only crayon drawings.
▪ Take your spring mural outside on a spring day. Attach the paper to the side of the building and provide children with tempera paints to work with. They can use the many "live models" around them as they paint a spring scene.

BOOKS

| Share these delightful spring books with fives. | ▪ *The Bear Who Saw Spring* by Karla Kuskin (Harper & Row) | ▪ *The Day the Sun Danced* by Edith Hurd (Harper & Row) | ▪ *The Rain Puddle* by Adelaide Hall (Lothrop, Lee & Shepard) |

ART

Discover the inventor in your fives!

INVENT A MACHINE

Aim: Children will use expressive language as they plan, construct, and describe their own machines.

Group size: Four to six children.

Materials: White glue, brass paper fasteners, masking tape, markers, scissors, shoe or cereal boxes, popsicle sticks, telephone wire, yarn, plastic foam pieces, paper plates, wood scraps, empty thread spools, cloth scraps, paper tubes, egg cartons, and any other odds and ends you have available.

GETTING READY

Invite children to talk about machines. Ask, "What is a machine? What can different machines do?" Record a list of machines children name on an experience chart. If possible, let children observe how some of the machines at school work, such as a copier, typewriter, or lawn mower.

BEGIN

Ask children to think about a machine they might like to invent. They can design it to do anything they want. For example, they might make a machine that puts away blocks at cleanup time or a machine that makes their bed at home.

Have each child choose one box as the base of the machine. They can use the glue, tape, and fasteners for attaching other objects to serve as parts. Use open-ended questions to help children develop ideas for their designs, such as, "How can a paper tube or a plate be used on your machine? What machine part does

this remind you of?" Be sure to let children create in their own ways. Their machines will make sense to them, even if they don't to you.

CREATE A "MACHINE MUSEUM"

Provide time for each child to describe his or her invention, telling you the name (if it has one), how it works, and where and by whom it would be used. Record each description on chart paper.

Choose a shelf or table to be the "Machine Museum." Display the machines, with the descriptions nearby. At circle time, give each child a chance to show and describe the invention to the others. If the children agree, try to arrange to have the machines displayed at a local library or in a merchant's window.

Remember

▪ Fives are fascinated by the way things work and like to experiment with tools and machines. Bring in a variety of old machines they can safely take apart and investigate. This exercise gives them a deeper understanding of how things work.

▪ Some items children want to put on their machines may be difficult to attach, offering wonderful opportunities for problem-solving. You might guide children with questions. For example: "Which do you think will work best — the tape, glue, or wire? Let's try one and see." But don't give the solution. Discovering it is part of the process.

BOOKS

Use these books about machines to introduce or follow up your machine-building.

▪ *Dig, Drill, Dump, Fill* by Tana Hoban (Greenwillow Books)

▪ *Simple Machines and How to Use Them* by Tillie S. Pine (McGraw-Hill)

▪ *The True Book of Toys at Work* by John Lewellen (Children's Press)

ART

Fives will enjoy this art activity with a sorting and classifying twist.

SORTING ART

Aim: Children will sort and classify objects before using them in an art project.

Group size: Four to six children.

Materials: Drawing or typing paper; old crayons with the paper coverings removed; tape; paper plates; objects for rubbings, such as coins, paper clips, buttons, corrugated cardboard, plaques or medals with raised letters, bark, cardboard shapes, letters, or stencils; and attribute blocks or paper shapes in three colors and shapes.

In Advance: Organize the art and sorting materials. Place crayons and papers in a bag or on a tray out of children's sight. Place objects for making rubbings on the art table, with paper plates for sorting them.

GETTING READY

Use attribute blocks or paper shapes to introduce the idea of sorting and classifying. Put out three paper plates. Choose one shape and ask one or more children to sort by color, placing the pieces of the same color on one paper plate. Then mix all the pieces together and have different children sort by shape.

BEGIN

Show children the different materials you have gathered, and invite them to name and describe each. Talk about how these materials might be sorted into different groups — such as by size, shape, texture, color, etc. Invite children to sort the objects onto paper plates, one plate for each classification scheme. As they work, encourage children to look for new ways to sort the objects, such as by things with letters and things without letters.

When the sorting is complete, distribute paper and crayons. Demonstrate how to make a kind of print of an object by placing it on the table, putting a piece of paper over it, then gently rubbing over the object with the side of the crayon in a back and forth motion. If necessary, use tape to hold the objects in place as children rub. You might model making rubbings of an entire sorted plate of objects, but let children choose whatever rubbings they want to make.

Remember

▪ Fives are at a stage of development where they understand sorting and classifying well enough to come up with their own classification schemes. However, it's still best to start with a simple sorting method, such as by size, color, or shape, before asking children to come up with their own ideas.

▪ Extend children's interest in rubbings by going on a "rubbing walk" to record different textures in nature. Label and display on a bulletin board. Invite families to go on "rubbing walks," and post their creations on your board.

BOOKS

Share these books on shapes and sizes at storytime.	▪ *Is It Larger? Is It Smaller?* by Tana Hoban (Greenwillow Books)	▪ *Shapes and Things* by Tana Hoban (Greenwillow Books)	▪ *What's Happening?* by Heather Amery (Usborne)

ART

Celebrate a windy day with homemade wind socks.

WE CAN CATCH THE WIND!

Aim: Children will use fine-motor, creative-thinking, and problem-solving skills as they make wind socks.

Group size: Four to six children.

Materials: Lunch-sized paper bags (one per child); colorful streamers or lightweight fabric strips; yarn, string, or twine; markers and crayons; masking tape; scissors; stapler; and an ornamental wind sock or a picture of one.

In Advance: Cut off the bottom of each paper bag so that it's open at both ends. Invite children who are adept at cutting to help with the process.

GETTING READY

Bring out this activity on a windy day. Ask, "How do you know when the wind is blowing? Can we see the wind? Can we feel the wind?" Together, observe the wind from a large window or doorway, or take a quick walk outside. Encourage children to watch for things they see that indicate the wind is blowing. Make an experience chart of their observations.

Then bring out your wind sock or a picture of one. Identify it and encourage children to tell anything they know about wind socks. Then ask, "What does a wind sock show you? How is it used?" Point out the long tails on the wind sock and ask, "What are these used for? How do you think they move in the wind?"

BEGIN

Now bring out the materials, and invite interested children to each make a wind sock. Have them decorate the paper bags with crayons or markers. Next, give them material strips or streamers to attach to one end of the bag with tape or staples. On the other end, help each securely tape one eight-inch piece of yarn or string to each corner of the bag. Tie the loose ends of all four pieces together, and then to that knot tie a longer piece of yarn for hanging.

Take the wind socks outside to test in the wind. You might tie them to tree branches or to playground equipment and watch them blow in the wind.

Remember

▪ You may notice that some fives are becoming interested in not only drawing or painting but in making something they can use. This activity is very satisfying for those children because the wind socks are relatively quick and easy to make and don't require children to make representational drawings.

▪ This project uses a good deal of tape. So that children don't have

to wait for you to hand out pieces of masking tape, cut many pieces in advance and attach to the side of the table. This allows children to work more independently.

▪ The lunch bags can also be used to create a kind of box kite. Do not cut off the bottoms. Attach the string and tails to the open end of the bags. When children run with the kite, the bag fills with air and should float.

BOOKS

| Share these books about the wind with fives. | ▪ *Fish in the Air* by Kurt Weise (Viking) | ▪ *Follow the Wind* by Alvin Tressalt (Lothrop, Lee & Shepard) | ▪ *Sailing with the Wind* by Thomas Locker (Dial Books) |

ART

Here's an activity that your budding architects will enjoy.

SHELTERS AROUND THE WORLD

Aim: Children will use problem-solving, observation, prediction, creative-thinking, and fine-motor skills as they design and build all kinds of houses.

Group size: Four to six children.

Materials: Assorted materials such as small boxes, paper tubes, plastic foam pieces, plastic containers, fabric and paper scraps, and straw; white glue; tape; crayons; markers; and pictures of different types of homes and housing all over the world. (Look for pictures in *National Geographic* magazines or in a Time/Life series on different regions of the world that is available in many libraries.)

GETTING READY

Gather children to talk about homes. Tell children about your home, and encourage them to describe their own. Make an experience chart from the information they share. Ask, "Why do people live in homes? Why don't we live in trees or in holes in the ground like some animals do?" Show children pictures of different kinds of homes in the United States and in other countries. Talk about how climate or available materials might determine the kinds of shelters people build. Compare homes in this country with homes in other places for similarities and differences.

BEGIN

Set out the materials you have gathered, and invite children to design their own homes. Display the pictures of homes to give children ideas, but be sure they understand that they can create any kind of home they want. Give children plenty of time for this project. Some may want to work on their shelters over several days, even bringing in items from their own homes to add to their designs.

TALK ABOUT IT, WRITE ABOUT IT!

When each home is finished, help the builder write (with inventive spelling) or dictate a story or description of the creation. Display the homes, with children's comments nearby. Provide time for each child to present his or her home to the others during circle time. Invite families to view the homes, too.

MAKE IT BIG!

As a follow-up activity, invite children to work together to turn a large appliance box into a kind of shelter. This new "home" can add an interesting dimension to children's dramatic play.

Remember

▪ Fives are developing a longer attention span and the ability to sustain interest in a project. It's important to periodically initiate projects that can take several days. Children will need this kind of concentration in the elementary grades.

▪ A great way to expand this activity is by studying different kinds of animal shelters. Investigate the various types: nests, hives, caves, webs, etc. Gather art materials children can use to build these different homes. Tap their imaginations by inviting children to make homes for imaginary creatures.

BOOKS

Share these stories that show a variety of settings.	▪ *Bringing the Rain to Kapiti Plain* by Verna Aardema (Dial Books)	▪ *The Crane Maidens* by Miyoko Matsutani (Parents Magazine Press)	▪ *People* by Peter Spier (Doubleday)

ART

Invite fives to title their pictures — just like great artists do!

THIS IS WHAT I'M GOING TO CALL IT

Aim: Children will use observation and language skills.

Group size: Four or five children.

Materials: Basic art materials such as tempera paints, watercolors, paper, crayons, construction paper scraps, marbles, file cards, and markers; and photos of famous impressionist and abstract paintings.

In Advance: Collect the paintings. Art magazines, old calendars, greeting and post cards, and library art books are all possible sources. Artists to look for include Monet, Klee, Miro, Mondrian, and Po!lack.

GETTING READY

Sharing examples of great abstract or impressionist art can help children to understand that a picture doesn't have to have recognizable figures. This can help them feel better about their own work.

Show children the pictures of paintings you have gathered. Explain that many artists give their work a title that describes what the artist is showing in the picture. Display the paintings one at a time, and invite children to suggest titles for what they see. Encourage them to use their imaginations and emphasize that there is no "right" answer. They can say whatever comes to mind. Record their ideas on chart paper, including the artist's title as the last entry. Check whether anyone came close to the artist's title. Discuss whether children think it's a good one. Then share other pictures and titles, helping children to find elements of the painting that the artist is describing in the title.

BEGIN

Now provide art materials for children to use in creating their own abstract art. For example, they might dip marbles in paint and roll them around on paper. They might paste geometric shapes onto paper for a collage effect or use watercolors to create a series of dots.

As children finish, ask them to study their artwork and to make up a title for each picture. Provide cards for them to write the titles using inventive spelling, or let them dictate the titles for you to record.

Display the masterpieces with titles tacked on nearby. Schedule time for each child to share his or her picture and title with the others.

Remember

▪ Once children get started titling their pictures, they often want to continue. Keep cards and markers near the easels so that children are free to title their work whenever they like.

▪ Some children will still respond with an "I don't know" when asked to title their pictures. Help these children by saying, "I don't know either, but let's do some pretending together. What does your picture make you think about?"

▪ Follow up this activity by having children brainstorm more unusual ways to create abstract art. For example, printing with gadgets, doing crayon resist, and "catching" paint bubbles on paper can all create interesting results and inspire titles.

BOOKS

Share these books about art and artists.

▪ *Ernie's Work of Art* by Valjean McLenighan (Sesame Street/Western)

▪ *Jackson Makes His Move* by Andrew Glass (Frederick Warne)

▪ *Marc Chagall, Artstart Very First Art Books* by Ernest Raboff (Doubleday)

ART

Bring snowy magic into your room, no matter what the weather outside!

A WINTER ART FESTIVAL

Aim: Children will use a variety of media and process art techniques to express visions of winter.

Group size: Four to six children.

Materials: Epsom salts, water, bowls, crayons, paintbrushes, dark-colored construction paper, plastic foam packing pieces, toothpicks, and box lids.

GETTING READY

Gather children together for a conversation about snow. Ask, "Does it snow where we live? If not, where do you have to go to find snow?" Talk about how snow looks, feels, smells, sounds, even tastes. Read a book with a snow theme, such as one below, and share the pictures of snowy scenes and activities.

BEGIN

Set up separate tables with each of the following activities. Children can move from table to table, experimenting with the materials available at each stop. The activities could also be done over several days, culminating in a "Winter Art Show."

SNOW-CRYSTAL PICTURES

First have children create the snow-crystal mixture. Mix 1/2 cup water with 1/2 cup Epsom salts. Stir well with a paintbrush. Make two bowls so there is one at each end of the table.

Give children dark-colored construction paper, such as blue, purple, or brown, to draw on with crayons. Encourage them to press hard on the crayons as they draw. When their crayon drawings are finished, have them paint over their scenes with the crystal mixture. (Have them always stir it first before painting.) Lay the papers flat to dry. When dry, children should see that crystals have formed to give the picture a sparkling-snow effect.

SNOW SCULPTURES

Place the plastic foam packing pieces and toothpicks in the center of a second table. Invite children to create their own snowflakes by connecting the packing pieces with the toothpicks. As they work, talk about the fact that no two snowflakes are alike, and encourage them to make any kind of shape they imagine. Display on dark paper or inside paper-lined box lids.

PUT ON AN ART SHOW

Arrange the finished snow art into an attractive display. Encourage children to write or dictate descriptions of their artwork or of the winter season to include in the display. Invite families to visit the group's Winter Art Festival.

Remember

▪ Fives are fascinated by snow and enjoy sharing their experiences playing in it or just watching snowflakes fall. Enhance language skills by encouraging children to write or dictate stories about snowy days.

▪ Let children create any kind of crayon scene they choose. Abstract designs will be just as intriguing covered with snow-like crystals as representational drawings.

BOOKS

Here are some wonderful books with snowy settings.

▪ *Biggest Snowstorm Ever* by Diane Paterson (Dial Books)

▪ *Josie and the Snow* by Helen Buckley (Lothrop, Lee & Shepard)

▪ *The Snowman* by Jon Orskine (Crown)

ART

Stimulate creative thinking and problem-solving with this open-ended art activity.

GRAB-BAG ART

Aim: Children will use a variety of art materials to create solutions to different types of problems.

Group size: Four to six children.

Materials: Lunch-sized paper bags; large paper plates; crayons or markers; white glue; plastic foam trays; index cards; assorted materials such as yarn, ribbon, fabric, and paper scraps; egg-carton cups; plastic foam packing pieces; clean milk cartons and margarine tubs; small boxes and paper plates; lids of various sizes; straws; cotton balls; tissues; and buttons.

In Advance: Fill a lunch bag for each child with an assortment of materials to inspire creative thinking. Each bag should have a different combination of materials. Be sure to include at least one large item — such as a milk container, plastic margarine tub, small box, or small paper plate — in each bag. This item will give each child something to use as a starting point for creating. Place a large paper plate under each bag to serve as the base for the artwork. Close each bag and mark with a giant question mark.

GETTING READY

Show children the grab bags. Explain that each is filled with surprise materials for making creations. To build excitement, encourage children to speculate about what might be in the bags.

BEGIN

Let each child choose a bag and give a tray to each. Have children dump the contents of their bags on the trays. Then present them with a problem to solve using the materials at hand. For example: "How can you use the objects in your bag to create something that flies? Or something that an animal lives in?"

Give children plenty of freedom to create in their own ways. Avoid offering suggestions unless a child specifically asks for help.

When children finish their creations, give each time to describe it to you or to the whole group.

Remember

▪ Enhance language development by encouraging children to write or dictate a description of their creation. You might place paper and writing tools near the art table for budding writers to use spontaneously.

▪ Consider repeating this activity around a particular theme. For example, when you are focusing on transportation, challenge children to make some kind of vehicle. Other themes might be animals, homes, monsters, people, etc. Ask children for their suggestions.

BOOKS

| Fives will enjoy these books with a creative twist. | ▪ *Daydreamers* by Eloise Greenfield (Dial Books) | ▪ *I Wish I Had a Computer That Makes Waffles* by Fitzhugh Dodson (Oak Tree Public) | ▪ *The Scribble Monster* by Jack Kent (Harcourt Brace Jovanovich) |

ART

Help bring Mother Goose characters to life for your children!

MOTHER GOOSE PUPPETS

Aim: Children will use creativity and expressive language as they make and use puppets.
Group size: Four to six children.
Materials: Newspaper, glue, tape, scissors, stapler, crayons, and heavy paper or oaktag; also see the materials list for each type of puppet.

GETTING READY

Introduce the activity with a puppet such as a Humpty Dumpty stick puppet you have created. Have the puppet talk to the children about different nursery-rhyme characters. Encourage children to ask questions about their favorite characters and recite their favorite rhymes. Read, recite, or dramatize different rhymes together. Then ask children to name characters they would like to make as puppets. Children who name the same characters may like to work together.

BEGIN

Show children the variety of materials available for making puppets. Encourage them to use creativity and language skills by discussing different ways to use the materials to make the puppets. Accept their ideas and offer these as well.

Stick Puppets: Children cut out magazine pictures or their own drawings of Mother Goose characters, then glue to heavy paper. Attach a tongue depressor or popsicle stick to the back of each for manipulating. Paper plates decorated with collage-material faces also make good stick puppets.

Mitten or Sock Puppets: Children stuff the end of an old mitten or sock with newspaper, then glue on fabric or yarn features and other details. Child inserts hand in mitten or sock to manipulate the puppet.

Ball Puppets: Make a hole in each of several small rubber or plastic foam balls for children. They glue on collage materials for features and yarn for hair. To use, a child places a fabric square over the pointer finger of one hand, then inserts the finger in the hole in the ball to manipulate the puppet.

Tube Puppets: Children use a paper-towel tube (cut in 3-inch lengths) for the body. They add features with markers or col-

lage-type items. Tape a popsicle stick inside the tube for manipulating the puppet.

IT'S SHOWTIME!

Help children construct a stage in the block corner by covering a large box or table with an old sheet or curtain. Ask each puppeteer to introduce his or her puppet to the group and tell which nursery rhyme it is from. Read the rhyme aloud, play a recording of it, or encourage the whole group to recite it as the puppeteers dramatize the action.

Remember

▪ Be sure children feel able to create Mother Goose characters in their own way, even if the finished products don't resemble the standard images.

BOOKS & RECORDS

These materials are great for puppet dramatizations.

▪ *The Gingerbread Man* by Karen Schmidt (Scholastic)

▪ *Tomie dePaola's Mother Goose* by Tomie dePaola (G.P. Putnam's Sons)

▪ *The Elves and the Shoemaker* retold by Freya Littledale (Scholastic Cassettes)

ART

Make interesting sounds with these colorful chimes!

LET'S MAKE WIND CHIMES

Aim: Children will use fine-motor skills and experiment with sound as they make wind chimes.

Group size: Four or five children.

Materials: Hard-plastic drinking cups; markers; aluminum foil; yarn; a cookie sheet; towels; a hammer; wooden branches, sticks, or dowels; and real wind chimes.

In Advance: You will need access to an oven, either one that's part of a stove or a portable toaster oven. To prepare, preheat the oven to its lowest temperature. Warn children to be careful around it.

GETTING READY

Bring out the wind chimes to show children. Talk about the sound the chimes make, and encourage children to describe it. Invite them to describe wind chimes they have at home.

BEGIN

Explain to interested children that they will be making wind chimes out of plastic cups. As part of the process, they will put the cups in an oven. Ask, "What do you think will happen when we put the plastic cups in the oven? How will they change? What do you think they'll look like after they've been in the oven?"

Give children the plastic cups and markers. Invite them to color the cups as desired. (If children are making individual chimes, each will need at least three cups. Or small groups can work together on chimes to keep in the room.) When the decorating is done, turn each child's cup upside down and place a towel over it. Using a hammer and nail, gently tap on the bottom until the cup is cracked. This will provide a hole for inserting string once the cups are melted.

Next, cover a cookie sheet with aluminum foil. Arrange the cracked cups upside down on the sheet. Place in the preheated oven and leave inside until the cups melt, just a few minutes. Watch them carefully. If your oven has a glass door, invite children to stand a safe distance away and observe the cups melting.

Remove the sheet from the oven. Let the cups cool about ten minutes, keeping out of children's reach.

When cool, have children insert colorful lengths of yarn through the holes in the now-melted cups. Tie the loose end of each piece of yarn to a branch or wooden stick. Place the cups close enough so that they will bump and "chime" in the wind. Tie an additional piece of yarn to the holder for hanging the chimes.

AN OVENLESS ALTERNATIVE

If you don't have access to an oven, use materials that can be easily strung and will make interesting noises when knocked together, such as small bells, metal bolts and washers, large seed pods, etc. Encourage children to bring in discards from home that they think will make good wind chimes.

Remember

▪ Encourage children to make large, solid blocks of color. Thin lines tend to get lost when the cup melts.

▪ Review safety rules for working around a warm appliance like the oven. Make sure children know not to touch it or the sheet of hot, melting cups. Remind children also that while you are melting the cups as a special project, they should never experiment with placing objects in their ovens at home.

BOOKS

Share these books about sounds with fives.

▪ *Crash! Bang! Boom!* by Peter Psier (Doubleday)

▪ *Lisa and Her Soundless World* by Edna Levine (Human Sciences Press)

▪ *Listen! Listen!* by Ann Paul Rand (Harcourt Brace Jovanovich)

ACTIVITY PLAN INDEX:
TWOS AND THREES

DEVELOPMENTAL AREAS AND SKILLS ENHANCED	Aesthetic Appreciation	Creative Expression	Social Interaction	Cooperation/Sharing	Science Concepts	Creative Thinking	Problem-Solving	Logic/Reasoning	Visual/Spatial	Using Language	Sequencing	Fine Motor
2'S ACTIVITY PLANS												
STICKY THINGS PAGE 38	■	■			■	■	■			■		■
FUN WITH PASTE AND GLUE PAGE 39	■	■				■	■		■	■		■
SAND, SAND, SAND PAGE 40		■			■	■				■		■
A TAPE-AND-STICK MURAL PAGE 41	■	■	■			■	■			■		■
FINGER-PAINT FUN PAGE 42	■	■	■		■			■		■	■	■
ALL KINDS OF BRUSHES! PAGE 43	■	■				■	■			■		■
CHALK SCRIBBLES PAGE 44	■				■					■		■
MAKING CUP TRAILS PAGE 45	■	■				■	■		■	■		■
PAINTING DAY PAGE 46	■	■	■		■					■		■
CRAYONS ARE FOREVER PAGE 47	■					■				■		■
3'S ACTIVITY PLANS												
PLAN A PURPLE DAY PAGE 48		■	■		■	■				■		■
COME TO OUR SIDEWALK ART SHOW! PAGE 49	■	■	■		■	■	■		■	■		■
EASEL EXCITEMENT PAGE 50	■	■	■			■	■		■	■		■
MAKE "SUN CATCHERS" PAGE 51	■	■	■		■				■	■	■	■
TRIPLE-FUN LEAF PRINTS PAGE 52	■	■	■		■	■				■	■	■
MONSTER MIX-UPS PAGE 53	■	■	■			■				■	■	■
MAGIC COLOR SPLOTCHES PAGE 54	■	■	■		■	■		■		■		■
SHARE COLORS WITH A FRIEND PAGE 55	■	■	■	■	■	■	■			■		■
LET'S MAKE A SPRAY-ART MURAL PAGE 56	■	■	■	■		■	■		■	■		■
CLOUDY-DAY PICTURES PAGE 57	■	■	■		■	■				■	■	■

ACTIVITY PLAN INDEX:
FOURS AND FIVES

DEVELOPMENTAL AREAS AND SKILLS ENHANCED	Aesthetic Appreciation	Creative Expression	Social Interaction	Cooperation/ Sharing	Science Concepts	Creative Thinking	Problem-Solving	Logic/ Reasoning	Visual/ Spatial	Using Language	Sequencing	Fine-Motor
4'S ACTIVITY PLANS												
ICICLE PAINTING PAGE 58		■	■		■			■		■	■	
OPPOSITE PRINTING PAGE 59	■	■	■			■			■	■	■	■
WIND-POWERED PAINTING PAGE 60	■	■	■	■	■	■	■	■	■	■		
SANDBOX ART PAGE 61	■	■	■	■	■	■	■	■	■	■	■	■
SNIP, SNIP, CUT, CUT PAGE 62		■	■			■	■		■	■		■
CRAYON-AND-PAPER BATIK PAGE 63	■	■	■		■					■		■
PLASTER SCULPTURE CREATIONS PAGE 64	■	■	■		■	■				■		■
IT'S RAINING RAINBOWS! PAGE 65	■	■	■	■	■	■		■		■		■
ART FOR A SUNNY DAY PAGE 66	■	■	■		■	■				■		■
CREATIVE FEATURES PAGE 67	■	■	■			■	■			■		■
5'S ACTIVITY PLANS												
A SPRING DAY MURAL PAGE 68	■	■	■	■	■	■	■	■	■	■		■
INVENT A MACHINE PAGE 69	■	■	■			■	■	■	■	■		■
SORTING ART PAGE 70	■	■	■			■		■	■	■		■
WE CAN CATCH THE WIND! PAGE 71	■	■	■		■	■	■			■	■	■
SHELTERS AROUND THE WORLD PAGE 72	■	■	■		■	■	■		■	■		■
THIS IS WHAT I'M GOING TO CALL IT PAGE 73	■	■	■			■			■	■		■
A WINTER ART FESTIVAL PAGE 74	■	■	■	■	■	■			■	■	■	■
GRAB-BAG ART PAGE 75	■	■	■			■	■		■	■		■
MOTHER GOOSE PUPPETS PAGE 76	■	■	■	■		■		■		■		■
LET'S MAKE WIND CHIMES PAGE 77	■	■	■		■	■			■	■	■	■

RESOURCES

Look for these materials to provide you with more ideas and a deeper understanding of how to help children engage in rich and creative open-ended art activities. Check for the books and articles in professional libraries or bookstores.

BOOKS

▼ *Active Learning for Twos* by Harms, Cryer, and Bourland (Addison-Wesley)

▼ *Art and Creative Development for Young Children* by Robert Schirrmacher (Delmar Publishers)

▼ *Clay in the Classroom: Helping Children Develop Cognitive and Affective Skills for Learning* by Sara Smilansky, Judith Hagan, and P. Helen Lewis (Teachers College Press)

▼ *Creative Art for the Developing Child: Teacher's Handbook for Early Childhood Education*, second edition, by Clare Cherry (Fearon Teacher Aids)

▼ *Don't Move the Muffin Tins: A Hands-Off Guide to Art for the Young Child* by Bev Bos (Turn-the-Page Press)

▼ *Infant/Toddler: Introducing Your Child to the Joy of Learning* by Earladeen Badger (McGraw-Hill)

▼ *Look at Me* by Carolyn Buhai Haas (CBH Publishing)

▼ *Learning Games for the First Three Years* by Joseph Sparling and Isabelle Lewis (Berkley Publishing)

▼ *Learning Games for Threes and Fours* by Joseph Sparling and Isabelle Lewis (Walker and Company)

▼ *1 2 3 Art* by Jean Warren (Warren Publishing House)

▼ *Scribble Cookies* by Ann F. Kohl (Gryphon House)

▼ *Teaching Terrific Twos and Other Toddlers* by Terry Lynne Graham and Linda Camp (Humanics Learning)

▼ *Things to Do with Toddlers and Twos* by Karen Miller (Telshare)

▼ *Total Learning: Developmental Curriculum for the Young Child,* third edition, by Joanne Hendrick (Merrill Publishing)

ARTICLES

▼ *"Creative Play"* by Sandra Waite-Stupiansky, Scholastic *Pre-K Today,* October 1990

▼ *"Creativity and How to Inspire It,"* by Bev Bos, Scholastic *Pre-K Today,* October 1988

▼ *"Kids & Art: Encouraging Self-Expression"* by Clare Cherry, Scholastic *Pre-K Today,* October 1988

▼ *"Outdoor Art: The Sky's the Limit"* by Dianne Jurek and Sharon MacDonald, Scholastic *Pre-K Today,* May/June 1990